W9-AYQ-564

Security and Environmental Change

Security and Environmental Change

SIMON DALBY

polity

Copyright © Simon Dalby 2009

The right of Simon Dalby to be identified as Author of this Work has been asserted in accordance with the UK Copyright, Designs and Patents Act 1988.

First published in 2009 by Polity Press
Reprinted in 2011

Polity Press
65 Bridge Street
Cambridge CB2 1UR, UK.

Polity Press
350 Main Street
Malden, MA 02148, USA

All rights reserved. Except for the quotation of short passages for the purpose of criticism and review, no part of this publication may be reproduced, stored in a retrieval system, or transmitted, in any form or by any means, electronic, mechanical, photocopying, recording or otherwise, without the prior permission of the publisher.

ISBN-13: 978-0-7456-4291-8
ISBN-13: 978-0-7456-4292-5(pb)

A catalogue record for this book is available from the British Library.

Typeset in 10.5 on 13 pt Minion
by Servis Filmsetting Ltd, Stockport, Cheshire
Printed and bound in the United States by Odyssey Press, Inc., Gonic, New Hampshire

The publisher has used its best endeavours to ensure that the URLs for external websites referred to in this book are correct and active at the time of going to press. However, the publisher has no responsibility for the websites and can make no guarantee that a site will remain live or that the content is or will remain appropriate.

Every effort has been made to trace all copyright holders, but if any have been inadvertently overlooked the publishers will be pleased to include any necessary credits in any subsequent reprint or edition.

For further information on Polity, visit our website: www.politybooks.com

Contents

Acknowledgments

Over the last few years many students in my "Environmental Geopolitics" course at Carleton University have engaged with the themes in this volume, and my thanks go to all of them for help in clarifying my ideas. Some of the ideas in this volume have also been presented to the International Studies Association as conference papers in 2002 and 2004, and to other academic and professional audiences in Kingston, Kathmandu, Melbourne, Ottawa, Toronto, Singapore, Chandigarh, Bern, Hamburg, and Vancouver. The Canadian Social Sciences and Humanities Research Council has supported my work over many years on a number of projects related to environment and security; I very much appreciate this institution's continued support of my scholarly efforts.

Iqbal Shailo and Susan Tudin provided invaluable research assistance in finding sources and tracking down elusive information. Ottawa colleagues Fiona Mackenzie, Nancy Doubleday, Mike Brklacich, Mike Pisaric, Matthew Paterson, Chris Burn, David Long, Graham Smart, James Meadowcroft, Patricia Ballamingie, and John Stone, as well as graduate students Andrew Baldwin, Jamie Linton, and Dale Armstrong in particular, have been most useful sounding boards for my ideas. Thanks too to Hans Guenter Brauch and Ursula Oswald Spring, whose ongoing collaboration has been so stimulating to my thinking in the last few years. My thanks also to Rita Floyd, Melanie Heintz, and Rachna Mishra for careful readings of the first draft of this book, and especially to Cara Stewart for her comprehensive editing of the text, and her crucial support at moments of authorly angst. Finally, my thanks to the Carnegie Council for permission to reprint material from my article, "Ecological Intervention and Anthropocene Ethics," which appeared as online exclusive in *Ethics and International Affairs* 21(3): 2007, and to all the staff at Polity for their careful work on this volume.

Abbreviations

AOSIS	Alliance of Small Island States
ENSO	El Niño Southern Oscillation
FAR	Fourth Assessment Report (of the IPCC, published in 2007)
GEO	Global Environmental Outlook
HESP	human and environmental security and peace
HUGE	human, gender, and environmental security
ICISS	International Commission on Intervention and State Sovereignty
IGBP	International Geosphere Biosphere Programme
IPCC	Intergovernmental Panel on Climate Change
MA	Millennium Ecosystem Assessment
MDG	Millennium Development Goals
NGO	non-governmental organization
RUSI	Royal United Services Institute
UNCHE	United Nations Conference on the Human Environment
UNDP	United Nations Development Program
WCED	World Commission on Environment and Development

Introduction: Change, Ecology, and Security

In the early years of the new millennium hurricanes lashed the Caribbean and, in the most high-profile case of Hurricane Katrina, flooded New Orleans. Heatwaves and floods seemed to alternate in Europe. Thousands died in the hot summer of 2003 in Paris while fires raged periodically across Greece and Portugal. Hollywood captured some of this worry about climate change in the 2004 disaster movie *The Day After Tomorrow*; Al Gore's documentary movie *An Inconvenient Truth* (2006) subsequently popularized the scientific case for concern and shared a Nobel peace prize with the Intergovernmental Panel on Climate Change (IPCC) in 2007. Snows were disappearing on Mount Kilimanjaro while the ice caps on both poles retreated. The North West Passage from the Atlantic through the Arctic to the Pacific was ice free for the first time in recorded history in 2007. People were in motion in many places seeking relief from disruptions of one form or another and apparently upsetting social stabilities in many places. The humanitarian disaster and ongoing war in Darfur in the first decade of the twenty-first century too were linked to environmental change and specifically climate-change-induced drought. Numerous thinktanks reported on the issue, once again linking the matter to the dangers of conflict and the possible security implications for many states with many "disasters." Charities and aid agencies also weighed in on the topic, concerned that climate change threatened the poor and marginal in new ways. Journalist Marq de Villiers summed up the doomsday tone of all this in his 2008 book simply titled *Dangerous World*.

Hanging over this discussion is an apocalyptic concern that humanity is destroying the biosphere, running amok on the only planet that is available for habitation. Pollution and the destruction of forests, looming shortages of petroleum and natural gas, of wheat and other essential grains, feed fears of the future and raise the specter of civilization as we know it disappearing altogether. Jared Diamond's bestselling book of 2005 examined the fate of previous societies that had disappeared, apparently as a result of resource and environmental difficulties, and did so with a title that bluntly caught the mood by phrasing matters simply in terms of *Collapse*. James Lovelock, the famous inventor of the concept of a self-regulating biosphere, "the Gaia Hypothesis" (Lovelock 1979), has recently suggested that we are moving into a period of great danger where human misdeeds have led to a situation in which we face *The Revenge of Gaia* (Lovelock 2006). Australian Friends of the Earth (Spratt and Sutton 2008), building on Lovelock's formulation, have invoked emergency medical terminology in declaring climate change a "code red" planetary emergency.

Facing such collapse surely is a matter that should invoke discussions of security, if not immediate emergency measures to change things and head off imminent dangers. However, who should act and how, and whether traditional notions of security have any relevance in these new circumstances, turn out to be much more complex than simple cries of "danger, do something" suggest. Traditionally national security has been about protection from external military threats or from internal subversion of the political order. The irony of climate change is that the threat is self-imposed; we are the makers of our own misfortunes. Or at least those of us who live in the prosperous, automobile- and airplane-addicted consumer societies of the planet are. If the poor subsistence farmers of Africa die from drought or flood, or the dwellers on atolls in the Pacific are overwhelmed by rising oceans, clearly they are not responsible for the disruptions and hence their fate. These are indeed externally caused security threats to the poor people living in vulnerable peripheries in the world system, caused by the rest of us. For all of us who write and read textbooks about security in particular, it is precisely this growth of the global economy that makes us affluent that is also changing planetary systems. This economic expansion has caused dramatic disruptions of natural systems in the search for ever larger supplies of minerals, fiber, food, and fuel, and the increased methane, carbon dioxide, and other greenhouse gases as a byproduct of transportation and industrial production. If these disruptions set the poor and marginal populations in the South in motion in search of food, shelter, jobs, and safety in the affluent North, then there is always the possibility that these people will be

portrayed as a threat to Northern societies "requiring" security measures to prevent their immigration. Some hard thinking is very much
in order here to address these issues, and this is what this book does.

Hence the title of this book can be read a number of ways. Most
obviously it suggests that security is being threatened by changes
in the natural environment. It is obvious because of the numerous
popular discussions of climate change, international debates about
the Kyoto Protocol and what comes after it, not to mention the intense
scientific activity investigating numerous aspects of the earth system.
The concern that drives all this activity and debate is precisely that
climate change and related phenomena are threatening to many ways
of life. Less obvious, but at least as important, is the opposite reading
of the title, the suggestion that environmental change might cause us
to rethink what we mean by security. This interpretation rests on the
irony that the social and political systems that have supposedly rendered at least the relatively affluent urban dwellers in the "Northern"
states secure have been based on the use of fossil fuels, which are now
disrupting the environment that gave rise to urban civilization in the
first place. In short, the question of which is securing what is not as
simple as the title of this volume might at first suggest.

Neither, as the first few chapters below outline, is this a very new
debate; scholars have been discussing all this under the heading of
"environmental security" for a couple of decades, although many of
the recent alarmist discussions of climate change causing conflict seem
to have forgotten much of this discussion. The scholarly literature that
suggests that environmental changes rarely cause conflict directly and
only occasionally do so indirectly (Kahl 2006) doesn't get as much attention in the media as the more alarmist claims about imminent crisis.
But nonetheless there are many reasons to be greatly concerned about
contemporary environmental changes and the potential they have to
render many people in many places insecure. As the book makes clear,
none of this has to lead to wars. Indeed thinking about security in new
ways that are not part of the legacy of Cold War concerns about military
preparation as security provision is an important part of what states,
societies, scholars, students, and citizens now need to do.

Much of the rest of this book is therefore about how we now think
about security and environment, both of which are changing in many

ways. How we use both of these terms is also changing, and clarity on this point is notably absent from policy debates and media commentary. Neither security nor environment is anything like as obvious as they once seemed. This is not a matter of clever plays on the meaning of words (Broda-Bahm 1999). It is about the now unavoidable realization that neither security, as we have traditionally understood it, nor environment, as we have usually taken it for granted, can continue to be interpreted or acted upon in traditional ways if either environmental change or security is to be thought about or made a political priority in useful ways for the majority of humanity or other species in coming decades (Barnett 2001). All this is so because humanity is changing what was once understood as an external environment, and in the process changing its circumstances of life in ways that make what is being secured increasingly artificial. Our thinking needs to catch up to this new reality.

Taking environmental change seriously requires us to rethink security quite dramatically. It might even mean that we should abandon it altogether; ecology, science, and history all point to the inevitability of change. Insofar as security is about making things, notably our consumer society, stay the same, it may in fact be part of the problem, rather than a way of thinking that is helpful in dealing with the future. Back in 1990 Daniel Deudney warned very clearly that military institutions in particular were frequently not the appropriate agencies for dealing with environmental issues. They are designed, equipped, and trained to break things and kill people, not nurture trees, breed fish, clean river beds, or install solar panels. Indeed the contemporary military use of fuels, chemicals, explosives, and radioactive substances makes them one of the most polluting of human institutions. Recently the 2007 United Nations Environment Program *GEO4* report on the global environmental outlook examined a number of scenarios of the future related to environmental change, and concluded that prioritizing security was nearly the worst possible way to proceed. But as the latter parts of this book discuss, some of the most alarming discussions about climate change and its consequences, and hence the need to take appropriate preventive action, are now coming from military thinktanks.

To think seriously about change and security it is necessary to consider history and the lessons that might be learnt from previous episodes of environmental disruption to societies (Diamond 2005; Linden 2007). If enough evidence exists concerning how they coped with disruptions then those are lessons that might have much to teach us. Whether the kind of violence and disruption that we now think about in terms of security were evident in earlier episodes, and if so where and when, these too might teach us very useful lessons. Many of the societies that became extinct have left few records from which it is possible to interpret how their debates went, whether the threats to the society were interpreted in ways that mirror our own concerns, and whether political strategies were tried and failed. But some archaeological reconstructions at least offer interesting hints. Large-scale disasters, short of complete destruction, offer more promising possibilities, especially where societies were literate and written accounts survive. Piecing together what evidence survives is a fascinating exercise in science, history, and archaeology, an exercise that may have some policy implications for our own societies in the present.

However, as this book suggests, these lessons are limited precisely because we have so dramatically changed human circumstances in the last few centuries, and especially in recent decades. As Jared Diamond (2005) observes, we can learn from earlier cases. More specifically, we might be able to learn useful lessons from the social traps that some earlier societies apparently were unable to evade as crisis and decline set in (Homer-Dixon 2006). But as chapter 3 shows, the most useful environmental history puts these changes into the appropriate context so that we understand the circumstances we have made, and hence how current vulnerabilities are now constituted.

Despite all the attention to climate change in recent years, focusing on it alone is insufficient. While atmospheric change and the increasingly rapid rise in global temperatures are very important, it is clear that these factors alone are not the whole story of the dramatic transformation of the earth's living systems that industrial civilization has set in motion. The rapid deforestation of the last few centuries, loss of many species, reduction in fish populations, conversion of huge areas to asphalt-covered cities, mining, farming, damming rivers, and numerous other activities are all happening at the same time. They are all having effects on how the biosphere behaves (Smil 2003). These factors need to be kept in mind when talking about environmental change, even if it's not always clear exactly how the different bits of the earth system fit together and how they may change as a result of human activities.

This discussion of earth-system science and the changing nature of the biosphere raises a crucial point that frequently reappears in the pages that follow. The sheer scale of the changes that have been set in motion now means that the conventional assumptions about environment as something out there, the given context for human affairs, is no longer a very useful way of thinking about present priorities. Precisely because of the disruptions set in motion by human activities, the distinction between culture and nature, human and environment, that has structured so much of the environmental discourse of the last century is becoming untenable. At the global scale we live in what might now more accurately be called a "social nature" (Castree and Braun 2001). Protecting nature, and seeing human actions as part of what has to be stopped to preserve nature, the logic of parks and conservation, is now no longer understood as either the only or the obvious way of proceeding. While "stopping the bulldozers" and declaring particular chunks of the biosphere "protected areas" are still important in many places, the larger questions of environmental change now suggest that such limited approaches to preservation are not anything like enough to deal with contemporary transformations.

The scientific recognition that environment as something external in need of protection is no longer an adequate formulation is now complemented by research in history and by political campaigns in the global South that have also repeatedly run up against the limits of this mode of thinking (Peluso and Watts 2001). The assumption of administrative areas that states should control to "protect" from people is a mode of thinking that runs back through the history of European state-making and the history of imperial administration (Scott 1998). Where parks were designated as royal hunting lands back in European history, the local residents who lived there suddenly became poachers and outlaws. Not surprisingly they resisted; the legend of Robin Hood tells an English version of the much larger story.

As European empires expanded in recent centuries, parks have frequently required the removal of local populations in the expansion of concerns with conservation areas and the maintenance of game reserves for the elites to hunt. Not surprisingly, people in the South react badly to Northern initiatives to set up international biosphere reserves and limit the use of land by indigenous residents; especially so when the "protected" wildlife threatens their lands and fields in ways that park administrators had mostly ignored until the last few decades (Adams and McShane 1992). Even then eco-tourism as a development strategy frequently trumps local subsistence activities. Only recently have many Northern environmentalists begun to understand this history and draw on the wider critical themes in earlier social thinking (Luke 1997) to rethink such projects as attempting to gain international sovereignty over the Brazilian rain-forest to "save" it from, well, Brazilians (Nordhaus and Shellenberger 2007).

But just as environment can no longer be taken for granted in discussions of environmental security, neither can security (Croft and Terriff 2000). During the Cold War national security relied on a fairly simple geography of protecting domestic spaces from external threats. In the aftermath of the Cold War this geopolitics is no longer useful; the cartography of danger changed (Shapiro 1997). Even the re-imposition of border controls and the discussions of "homeland security" in the "war on terror" are tied to a discussion of globalization as the source of terrorist threats. Security is not just about threats, armies, and government policies dealing with conflict. It now encompasses broader concerns with security, health, drugs, political violence, livelihoods, and infrastructure.

Most of these themes are part of what became known as "human security" in the 1990s United Nations Development Program formulation (UNDP 1994), when threats to people became the focus, and inter-state wars were assumed to be much less of a concern than in the Cold War period. More recently, and of particular importance for the themes of this book, when human security is put at the heart of the analysis and linked to both the science of earth systems and the historical lessons about how people die in disasters, then a different set of security priorities becomes apparent (Brauch 2005a, 2005b). But whether these formulations will shape policy, or whether older formulations of security predicated on protecting the existing social order against disruptions win out, is a crucial matter of geopolitics in the coming decades.

This in turn once again raises questions of who security is for, and what circumstances are designated as a threat to that security. It makes unavoidable the question of what social order is being secured for the future (Dalby 2002). Security has been invoked frequently in the past as a response to numerous threats of many kinds in many circumstances. Alarms about population and resources are not new either; Thomas Malthus' (1798/1970) *Essay on the Principle of Population* has been read for two centuries, while human population and its mode of subsistence have expanded in ways that were inconceivable to the author writing at the beginning of the industrial revolution. The modes of thinking from earlier episodes may have useful lessons to teach about how we now think about security; but unless they are appropriately put into context they may simply be misleading.

The irony of considering security as threatened by change is also worth considering. After all, our whole society seems to be run on new and better things. Diseases that killed our grandparents are now curable. Air pollution in big cities in many parts of the world is reduced, although Chinese cities in particular still face many problems of air quality. The dangers of war between states, the classic problem of security studies, are supposedly now reduced to a matter of peripheral states in the world system, not a matter for metropolitan societies. In everyday life things are much improved, and for all the concern expressed in the media about technological threats of various kinds, the practical innovations of technology seem to have improved our lives considerably. CDs long ago replaced records, and are now being replaced by downloadable files, MP3 players and iPods. HDTV promises digital experiences that mere television could never offer. Cars have ever more sophisticated technologies and old-fashioned maps are now being replaced by GPS. We live longer than our parents' and much longer than our grandparents' generation did on average. Big homes, miraculous communication technologies, hygiene and medical improvements have all opened up numerous new possibilities. Growth is apparently a good thing in at least most matters; scarcity has been effectively banished for many of the rising middle classes in developing countries, only most obviously China and India. Huge numbers of people now travel round the world each day in airplanes, a technology that is only a century old. Hasn't change made many people much more secure in many senses in the last while, as Bjorn Lomborg (2001), in particular, has repeatedly argued? Globalization may bring uncertainty, but it also brings vacations in exotic spots, foods and music from round the world into our lives in ways that supposedly makes us much more fulfilled as human beings than earlier generations. So why might change, even environmental change, then be a problem for security?

Clarity and careful analysis are needed here too to make sense of what it is that is endangered, and how such threats are invoked in the very political language of security. The climate-change debate has come to dominate these discussions in the last few years; 2007 may well turn out to be a turning point, as environmentalist Nick Mabey (2007) suggests in his sobering analysis published by a British military thinktank. Alarm about climate change and related disasters is certainly not in short supply, as numerous recent popular books attest (Flannery 2006; Monbiot 2006; de Villiers 2008; Weaver 2008). But putting all this into the appropriate context needs a focus on the conceptualizations of both security and environment, and attention also to history and to science, as well as some careful reflection on the geography of all this in terms of who lives where and is hence vulnerable to what forms of insecurity.

To make sense of all these matters the rest of the volume is divided into six substantive chapters and a brief conclusion.

Chapter 1 looks back to past thinking about fears related to environmental matters, starting with Thomas Malthus, who usually gets all the blame for scarcity narratives, and deals next with the 1970s limits-to-growth debate. Many of the themes from the 1970s are back in the current debate, and reminding ourselves of these earlier discussions is important so that lessons can be learned and unfounded claims to novelty rejected. Later sections show how some of the Malthusian themes reappeared in the 1990s discussion about environmental security that was especially prominent in Robert Kaplan's (1994) much-cited dystopian essay "The Coming Anarchy." The doom and disaster that Kaplan portrays is topped only by the literature that suggests the imminent end of civilization as a result of climate change.

Which leads to a second chapter, on the larger questions of how security should and might be reformulated since the nuclear standoff between the superpowers ended. Who is insecure how and where are key to this discussion, but the conceptualizations of security remain a matter of political order and state power even when pressing priorities of disease, water supplies, and environment appear to be more immediately endangering people in many places. The human-security agenda is important in changing the focus from states, borders, and national security and in challenging simple assumptions that environmental change causes violence. But concepts of danger and nature are part of the cultures that are apparently threatened, and the politics of invoking security is an important part of this whole discussion.

Third, precisely because environmental change is caused by human action it is important to engage the literature on environmental history, which has explored the collapse of earlier civilizations and the important disruptions of earlier empires and the environmental contexts that made them possible. There may be all sorts of lessons to be learned, but few of the historians who write on this matter engage concepts of security very directly, so lessons need to be extracted carefully. However, historians have been hard at work of late linking matters of economic change with environment and resource extractions. Building on work by Alfred Crosby, in particular in his 1986 book *Ecological Imperialism*, the connections between human activity and environmental change are now clearly understood as intricately interwoven. Indeed the relationships between science and disaster, and in particular blaming nature for disasters that are at least partly a matter of human actions, are also tied up with the disruptions wrought by the dramatic expansion of the global economy in the last couple of centuries. Imperial expansion in the late nineteenth century is related to the huge famines that swept Asia and Africa in particular. Variable rainfall, being measured by the new science of meteorology, suggested a stingy and capricious nature was to blame for famine, rather than imperial political economy. Linking famines to the global political and economic system is essential to put this all into the appropriate ecological context.

The fourth chapter deals in more detail with ecological science, and in particular the current earth-system science investigations, which are making it clear that humanity is changing its habitat in unpredictable ways that need to be thought about carefully if the future is to be part of a recrafted conceptual and policy agenda. Getting the science right has been a major problem in the literature on environmental security for the last two decades (Sullivan 2000) and this science on the big scale makes it both more difficult and more important. Recent overviews of ecological and climate matters do make the picture much clearer. Arguments about climate change are now emerging as the dominant theme in these discussions, and ones that apparently might have dramatic security implications. In particular it is important to look at how complex systems change, and how human and ecological systems are interconnected. The sheer scale of human activities means that we are living in increasingly artificial circumstances in a biosphere that we are changing. This is in effect a new geological period called, following Paul Crutzen's (2002) suggestion, "the Anthropocene," shaped in novel ways by the human factor in planetary matters.

It is precisely the perturbations in the earth system that are induced by human actions that compose the global urbanized economic conditions of humanity, which are the most likely cause of environmental harm that will affect both human and national security in the foreseeable future. This theme is covered in chapter 5. Now that we are living in the Anthropocene, human actions are a part of the biosphere; environment is no longer an external agent in human affairs. The implications of this are profound, not least in that we have to think about the mundane details of everyday life in the global economy as shaping the future of the planet. Not the kind of thing that most scholars or students are used to doing, or what security analysts usually do! But the rise in the number of casualties from disasters round the world, and the failure of emergency systems to deal with many aspects of Hurricane Katrina in particular, make it clear that human vulnerability especially to storms, heatwaves, droughts, and hurricanes has to be part of the security agenda now. But how security is invoked, and precisely what is designated as the threat, is an unavoidably political exercise, as this chapter shows in a discussion of New Orleans and a major rainstorm that struck the Indian city of Mumbai a month before Katrina.

Sixth, in light of these discussions of history, science, and vulnerability we need to think again about the possibilities of human security, and preparations to deal with environmental disruptions, when they occur, as a constructive initiative in global security that can promote cooperation rather than conflict in the face of disaster, while simultaneously reducing the total impact of human activity on the biosphere. To do so requires us to challenge the view from the metropoles, the imperial administrator's view of the world where Northern forces might need to intervene in the South to deal with environmental emergencies, because on the biggest scale of climate change it is now clear that alarm about this issue is finally making military institutions pay serious attention to global order and the unsustainable global economy. Climate change is also beginning to shift the geopolitical sensibilities from matters of protecting borders to thinking about global interconnections and the fact that affluence is making the poor and marginal insecure. The good news is that some ideas about sustainable security are on the policy agenda and possibilities for rethinking security are being canvassed now that the failures of the policies of the "war on terror" are becoming unavoidable.

The book's conclusion then suggests that earlier concerns about scarcity are of much less relevance than the need to think and plan for security in ecological terms in the Anthropocene. Looking at the larger intellectual context within which security is situated suggests that the conceptual categories that we use to think about both environment and security need some fundamental overhauls; matters environmental activists and military thinkers are both addressing in parallel. All of which makes the debates about human security much more interesting as they engage the contemporary literature on earth-system science rather than traditional environmental literature about parks, wilderness, and "protecting nature."

Taking ecological thinking seriously suggests the possibilities for reducing vulnerabilities while simultaneously rethinking how security is understood. What a sustainable security policy might look like in the face of environmental change on the largest scale is very difficult to specify in detail, but the general outlines of what needs to be done, and how security should be rethought in these circumstances, is becoming much clearer as a result of the debates of the last few decades. The book concludes with some reflections on this agenda for the future.

1

Environmental Fears: From Thomas Malthus to Ecological "Collapse"

Much environmental thinking doesn't explicitly deal with matters of security, even in the early literature where technological dangers supposedly required emergency measures. Nonetheless it is important to think about how the whole notion of environment has developed and how conceptualizations of nature and resources have come to shape the debate now that security has been directly linked with "environment." Most important are the practices of modern administration and their formulation of problems in such a way that they present us with an environment that needs to be controlled, regulated, legislated, governed, and now apparently "secured" (Dalby 2002). This political history affects how we think about what needs to be done by whom in the face of apparent threats to many things. Once one looks at environment in these terms it quickly becomes apparent that threats and their representation are a crucial part of the discussion. Fears of all sorts of biological threats, poisons and pollution, terrorist actions, and invasions by foreigners are linked into anxieties about security that are especially prevalent in the era of the "war on terror" (Hartmann et al. 2005). This is part of complex cultural processes of fear and politics that only sometimes link environmental matters to security.

This chapter deals with only some parts of the history of environmental thinking, how threats needing international responses became part of political vocabulary, and how shifting interpretations of the importance of environment as a priority became part of governmental activities and core themes in the non-governmental organizations (NGOs), civil society organizations, and foundations that form the broad and diverse movement that is often lumped together under the label of "the environmental movement." (See O'Riordan 1976; Sandbach 1980; Luke 1997, 1999.) How all this feeds into the matter of security as such is discussed in more detail in chapter 2;

environmental matters aren't necessarily of concern to security specialists, or a matter of state priorities in terms of national security. Indeed, as will be made clear later in this book, there are some compelling arguments against invoking security discourses in dealing with environmental matters. But first, and all too briefly, some of the salient themes in environmental arguments need to be presented, and the current worries over climate change and large-scale dangers to the biosphere put in their historical context.

More specifically, this chapter deals with articulations of environmental matters and danger. Hence it starts with a brief discussion of Thomas Malthus, whose essay on population, penned two centuries ago, is usually understood as the key text in the modern debate about resources and scarcity and the supposed dangers of overpopulation. Many of these themes were discussed at length in the late 1960s and early 1970s, when "the population bomb" was linked to larger concerns about resources and environment. The debate about "the limits to growth" was accentuated when, in the aftermath of the October 1973 war between Syria, Egypt, and Israel, a number of oil embargos resulted and the Organization of Petroleum Exporting Countries (OPEC) hiked prices (Yergin 1991). Shortages of fuel suggested the arrival of resource scarcity. In subsequent years as supplies were diversified prices once again declined and attention focused on other matters. The 1970s were also a decade marked in many industrial states by sustained efforts to reduce the most obvious and dangerous forms of pollution. Earlier alarms were partially addressed in legislation and by the apparent export of some of the dirtiest industries to poorer parts of the world economy.

Environmental matters returned to the international agenda in the late 1980s, when the Chernobyl nuclear reactor meltdown, ozone holes, burning rainforests, and the hot summer of 1988 focused attention as the Cold War subsided. Then the links between security and broadly defined environmental matters were explicitly drawn with much greater scope than the earlier concerns with resource supplies in the mid-1970s (Dalby 2002). The larger discussions of sustainable development linked up with a discussion of new threats to security. This political concern fed into the huge United Nations Earth Summit in Rio de Janeiro in 1992 without much explicit attention to these matters in terms of environmental security. Eighteen months after the summit Robert Kaplan's widely cited cover story on "The Coming Anarchy" in the February 2004 issue of the *Atlantic Monthly* magazine focused attention on the links once more.

In the second half of the first decade of the twenty-first century these matters are now pressing priorities in political discussions. Many international reports, scientific studies, and policy analyses have focused attention on climate change in particular and related matters of biodiversity loss, the extinction of species, and once again concerns about peak oil and the exhaustion of supplies of cheap petroleum. Overarching this is a discussion of major disasters and the possibility of the end of contemporary civilization; the theme of Jared Diamond's (2005) bestselling book *Collapse*. However, just as environmental changes are being caused by our current activities, we are also changing both our capabilities and the context in which we face these challenges. Humanity is increasingly in charge of its own fate.

Clearly the contemporary climate crisis in particular suggests we have much to learn, and need to learn it quickly. As will become clear in the rest of this book, not only is environmental change happening at an increasing pace, but how we understand the environment has also changed very substantially in the last few decades. We now know much more than we did in the early 1970s when alarm about environment was first on the political agenda. In the process, thinking has gradually shifted from environment as an external entity to be managed to a recognition of the affluent part of humanity as the maker of our collective fate.

That is not quite how things looked two centuries ago through the eyes of Thomas Malthus, however, and many of his concerns are remarkably persistent in arguments about how environment should be linked to security. As later sections of this book make clear, alarm about population, environmental scarcity, and threats that are caused by these things are frequently misleading when climate and other forms of environmental change are linked into security discussion. However, given the persistence of Malthusian formulations in contemporary thinking, his legacy needs to be briefly discussed first.

Thomas Malthus, Population Bombs, and the Limits to Growth

Thomas Malthus frequently gets most of the blame for tales of woe related to environmental matters. The country parson who became one of the first professional economists has given his name to a whole mode of thinking that continues to shape a substantial part of how we talk about what is now called environment. The term "Malthusian" is part of the English vocabulary in most parts of the world. In his lifetime Malthus' (1970) most famous essay, "On the Principle of Population," appeared in a number of editions (starting in 1798), and it changed as he refined his thinking and responded to his critics. But few people now go back to read what he had to say. Instead the central theme of scarcity as a limit on humanity's potential has been adopted as part of modern political argument and economic reasoning (Xenos 1989), and Malthus' name has been repeatedly attached to arguments about a stingy nature as the cause of much human misery and environmental conflict (Urdal 2005). Above all, Malthus' argument is remembered as suggesting that we breed faster than we can expand our abilities to feed ourselves and so we ensure that misery persists. This propensity can be tackled, Malthus thought, through moral reform and sexual abstinence, or more recently, through the adoption of birth-control methods, on the part of those who previously supposedly bred too enthusiastically.

Malthus' concerns were also within a larger geopolitical imagination of the world where breeding and population were understood as a threat to particular polities. Larry Lohmann (2005), in an essay tracing the history of the connections between fears of scarcity and geopolitics, opens his discussion reprinting a passage from the "Essay on the Principle of Population": "clouds of Barbarians seemed to collect from all points of the northern hemisphere. Gathering fresh darkness and terror as they rolled on, the congregated bodies at length obscured the sun of Italy, and sunk the whole world in universal night. These tremendous effects . . . may be traced to the simple cause of the superior power of population to the means of subsistence" (Malthus 1970: 83). Fear of Asian hordes overrunning Europe, and of the lack of available "manpower" to protect Rome, or later the

British empire, from external threats, is a persistent part of geopolitical discourse (Kearns 2009), and one that is reprised in discussions of Eurabia, Islam, and the threats to European civilization to this day. As Lohmann (2005) puts it, these Malthusian fears are not usually about us but about "them," the poor and the foreign, who breed too profusely for "our" comfort.

There is another aspect to Malthus too: the economist and mathematician concerned to apply policies that would solve all sorts of social problems, but who usually took the operation of the market society and the institutions of that society for granted, as something beyond discussion, rather than as the source of many of the problems which he wished to address. He was most concerned about the ability of society to feed itself, a matter of the limited, as he saw it, ability to expand production fast enough to feed a growing population. His critics, from the nineteenth-century political economists, only most famously Karl Marx, to more recent writers, have long focused on the economic sources of poverty rather than the supposed natural limits to subsistence (Eric B. Ross 1998).

While many of the original arguments about the ability of societies to feed themselves were demolished by the end of the nineteenth century, and the dramatic changes that the industrial revolution wrought suggested that humanity was capable of extraordinary expansion, the fear of living beyond the capabilities of environmental resources has remained a powerful theme in political discourse and was especially so in the 1970s (Harvey 1974). Demography, even before it became a science of that name, was a persistent theme in discussions of colonial administration in the British empire in particular, where questions of managing populations in the colonies were never far from administrators' minds (Grove 1995, 1997). Here the natives were frequently understood as a threat to the imperial order or at least to its administration in a manner that ensured essential commodities were produced and exported in an orderly manner. Where Malthusian arguments operate to suggest that marginal and poor people are the source of difficulties for the rest of us, they frequently obscure matters of wealth distribution (G. Williams 1995). Likewise the supposed irrationalities of the poor and marginal, when judged through the lenses of colonialism, or more recently state development discourses, frequently occlude what might be sensible strategies if viewed through the lenses of the poor and marginal.

Extended into discussions of resources other than food, in various forms of neo-Malthusianism, the argument reiterates concerns about the limits of human capabilities. If the world is running out of copper, iron, or, perhaps most ominously for contemporary car drivers (Urry 2008), petroleum, then the limits to industrial growth and the potential for expansion of consumer societies once again loom. Given how widespread plastics and petroleum-based materials are in contemporary civilization, petroleum is especially relevant to this discussion. Much less reflected upon in most neo-Malthusian arguments is the necessity of using specific resources for certain modes of living. In a society not addicted to the private automobile and with heating systems and machinery fueled in other ways, scarcity of petroleum isn't a threat. Resources are tied into particular ways of life; flint isn't in short supply these days because no one "needs" it to make arrow heads.

In the 1960s as rapid population growth occurred round the world, Thomas Malthus was dusted off in a discussion of how all these new mouths would be fed. Paul Ehrlich (1968) published a small popular book simply called *The Population Bomb*. Extrapolating into the future, he suggested that famine was inevitable as the growing numbers of poor people in particular were unlikely to be fed. Shortages of land, fertilizers, and other inputs suggested that the planet could not feed the growing numbers in the future. However, many alarmist arguments were in part countered by technological innovations and the adoption of new food crops of the so-called green revolution. Hybrid varieties of wheat and rice emerged from research programs where science met agriculture and productivity increased. Mechanized farming, fertilizers, and technological innovations expanded food supplies, and while many people did starve, in Africa in particular, in subsequent decades the numbers of humans continued to expand, albeit at slower rates than the alarmist accounts of the 1960s suggested were likely.

Shortly after *The Population Bomb* was published, early computer scenarios of the future began to be generated, in particular by a project commissioned by the Club of Rome on the predicament of humankind. Titled *The Limits to Growth*, the report, first published in 1972, left little doubt about its findings. It extended concerns with food and population to the larger context of humanity's future. The project built a formal mathematical model of the world "to investigate five major trends of global concern – accelerating industrialization, rapid population growth, widespread malnutrition, depletion of non-renewable resources, and a deteriorating environment" (Meadows et al. 1974: 21). While recognizing the limits of the model and suggesting that future improvements would be necessary as better data on the world's attributes became available, the project nonetheless suggested that the model was robust enough and the analysis important enough to bring it out of the computer lab at the Massachusetts Institute of Technology and publish it for a general audience.

The three key findings of *The Limits to Growth* report were clear about the choices facing humanity, and the ominous fate awaiting us if then current trends were not changed:

1. If present growth trends in world population, industrialization, pollution, food production, and resource depletion continue unchanged, the limits to growth on this planet will be reached sometime within the next one hundred years. The most probable result will be a rather sudden and uncontrollable decline in both population and industrial capacity.
2. It is possible to alter these growth trends and to establish a condition of ecological and economic stability that is sustainable far into the future. The state of global equilibrium could be designed so that the basic material needs of each person on earth are satisfied and each person has an equal opportunity to realize his individual human potential.
3. If the world's people decide to strive for this second outcome rather than the first, the sooner they begin working to attain it, the greater will be their chances of success. (Meadows et al. 1974: 23–4)

While the authors didn't use the phrase "sustainable development," it's clear that the second finding here is one that is loosely similar to what has subsequently been adopted under this rubric.

Critics were quick to pounce on some of the limits of the model. An edited volume from authors based at the Science Policy Research

Unit at the University of Sussex challenged such *Models of Doom* and the assumptions of both social and technical change that underlay the pessimism of *The Limits to Growth*'s first conclusion (Cole et al. 1973). The first chapter in this volume is appropriately titled "Malthus with a Computer." As the growing concern over climate change suggests, the authors turned out to be right about at least one limit, that of the atmosphere to absorb one particular kind of pollution: carbon dioxide. Interestingly, the volume ends with a discussion of the basic views of humanity that drive such exercises, contrasting a "Western" perspective, wherein humanity's intellect allows for progress and the exploitation of the whole planet for humanity's wants, with an "Eastern" perspective, wherein humanity is part of an intricate web of life within which we exist. In short, the criticisms focus on the political assumptions that drive such thinking and raise the possibilities of thinking beyond the Western instrumental view of things. This criticism has now ironically been reinforced by Western science and the use of huge new climate computer models, much more sophisticated than their precursors in the 1970s, which are making it ever clearer that we live within a system which our "instrumentalism" is now fundamentally changing.

In 1972 too the United Nations organized the first international conference on environment in Stockholm. Formally called the United Nations Conference on the Human Environment (UNCHE), it drew few heads of state to the meetings, was boycotted by Soviet bloc states, but did raise numerous important questions about the future and human institutions. The background volume written for the conference by Barbara Ward and Rene Dubos (1972) and published as *Only One Earth* used the theme of "the care and maintenance of a small planet" as its subtitle. Looking back, it is interesting to note that there are discussions of problems of "coexistence in the technosphere" and "strategies for survival" but few invocations of either a global problem or managerial approaches to the issues. Editors of the *Ecologist* (Goldsmith et al. 1972), then a new magazine in Britain, caught the mood of the times and issued *A Blueprint for Survival* incorporating scientific arguments that were broadly similar to those of *The Limits to Growth*. They also suggested that smaller-scale communities relying on local resources were much more likely to be sustainable and humane than large-scale industrial metropoles with their huge resource consumption.

Sustainable Development and Environmental Security

In many parts of the Third World, oil-price hikes in the 1970s in the aftermath of the October 1973 war between Syria, Egypt, and Israel, which triggered oil embargos by a number of oil-producing states, had damaging effects on development, and the debts rapidly accumulated as economies that had just begun to become dependent on oil imports suddenly had to pay much higher prices. When these factors linked up with Northern discussions of the limits to growth and the claims of a need for conservation and limits on production, many Third World politicians interpreted this as an attempt on the part of affluent Northern governments to keep the advantages they had gained over previous centuries of imperial rule for themselves and to restrict Southern development. Not surprisingly such suggestions were vehemently opposed, notably at the 1972 Stockholm UNCHE meeting, but also later in numerous international meetings where politicians in the South were much more concerned that Northern states live up to their commitments to aid in Southern development, or, where they agreed to forgo technologies such as chlorofluorocarbons, that Northern states provide financial compensation to facilitate producing alternatives (Kjellen 2008).

Perhaps nowhere was this more so than in Brazil, where politicians, and the military rulers during the period of their dictatorship in particular, eyed the Amazon region as a huge, untapped reservoir of resources that would allow Brazil to develop in a manner analogous to the United States by opening up the interior to farming and mining. Environmentalists from around the world did not seem to understand why the Brazilian government repeatedly invoked claims of sovereignty and portrayed environmentalists, who went to the Amazon to "save" it from Brazilians, as a threat to national security (Nordhaus and Shellenberger 2007). Claiming the national territory of another state as a matter of a common heritage of humanity looks very like earlier imperial claims on resources and territories in the name of empire, civilization, or Christianity.

The most notable effort in the 1980s to deal with all these issues was the World Commission on Environment and Development (WCED 1987), which worked to find compromise positions on these conflicting positions. Its final report on *Our Common Future*, frequently known as the Brundtland report after the commission chair Gro Harlem Brundtland, popularized the term "sustainable development" as a compromise position. The key innovation is linking environmental concerns with the necessity to confront poverty. This is effectively an attempt to answer arguments that the North had got rich exploiting the resources of the planet and the South was never going to agree to remain in poverty as the price of "saving" a world that they had not damaged (Agarwal and Narain 1991). Neither, so the arguments at the time went, were Southern elites going to forgo the prosperity of development on the basis of alarmist scenarios, most of which did not foresee the rich and powerful making real efforts to address the gross inequities in the world. Numerous statements about aid and development were made in the United Nations in the 1960s and 1970s, but few Northern states followed through on their commitments. Where they had done so many of the benefits were obliterated by rising fuel prices in the 1970s and the need for Southern states to borrow to pay the bills. This in turn led to the debt crisis, in which poor states effectively returned aid payments in the form of interest payments on their national debts many times over (George 1988).

Our Common Future was published the year after the world had once again been reminded of the dangers of nuclear fallout as a result of the disaster at the Chernobyl nuclear reactor in the Soviet Union. Clouds of radioactive contamination drifted over Russia and Scandinavia before spreading further afield. Reindeer in Sweden and Finland were contaminated for years afterwards and the failure of national boundaries to provide any security from disasters was once again emphasized. The failure of the Soviet Union to deal effectively with the disaster, and the clear indication that covering up and denying what was happening was no longer a politically acceptable option, fueled "Glasnost" in Moscow and fed into the radical rethinking of security that was then underway as the dangers of nuclear war and the possibilities of political accommodation with the United States were explored. In the words of Eduard Sheverdnadze, then the Soviet foreign minister, "For the first time we have understood clearly what we just guessed: that the traditional view of national and universal security based primarily on military means of defense is now totally obsolete and must be urgently revised" (as cited by Dabelko 2008: 36). The Soviet Union explicitly raised matters of the international environmental dimensions of security in the United Nations in the late 1980s. But these ideas were quickly discounted by the United States in particular, with counterarguments focusing on the abysmal record of the Soviet Union on environmental matters being used in the dismissal. The fact that the accident at Chernobyl might have caused a fundamental rethink of security in Moscow wasn't taken seriously at the time. Likewise, proposals paralleling the traditional United Nations "blue helmets" peacekeeping missions with a "green helmets" environmental intervention force to deal with environmental difficulties were dismissed, not least by Southern states invoking sovereignty and the non-intervention norm to reject what they saw as one more Northern justification for intervention (Dabelko 2008).

As the Cold War came to an end, it coincided with a new round of concern about environmental matters and new forms of threat discourse. Huge fires in the Amazon forests suggested major destruction of ecosystems there, although the precise pattern of development that led to these fires wasn't initially clear (Hecht and Cockburn 1990). The summer of 1988 was especially hot and dry in the United States and the commercial shipping on the Mississippi river was disrupted because of low water levels. James Hansen, a leading climate scientist in the United States, gave testimony in the United States Congress to the effect that there now was a discernible warming of the planet and that it was fairly clear that human actions were part of that warming (Schneider 1989). A major international conference on "The Changing Atmosphere: Implications for Global Security," in Toronto in 1988, coupled discussions of stratospheric ozone depletion with growing concern over climate change. In the aftermath of the Bhopal chemical plant disaster in India, which had killed thousands in 1984, and the fallout from Chernobyl too, a global sense of crisis pervaded media commentary. *Time* magazine replaced its person-of-the-year item with the endangered planet in its 1989 cover story of the year. *Scientific American* published a special issue on "Managing Planet Earth." All fed into rising concern with environmental matters. The IPCC was established to evaluate the science on climate change and clarify what was known and what wasn't in a way that could usefully feed into international discussion of the topic; its first assessment appeared in 1990.

A number of authors explicitly linked environmental difficulties with the end of the Cold War by arguing that environment was the new threat that had to be dealt with. What has become the discourse of environmental security came from this period, in which policy discussions linking environment explicitly with traditional priorities of security routinely appear in public discussions and policy debates. *Our Common Future* had included the assumption that conflict would result from growing scarcities of resources; indeed it was one of the arguments for the necessity of thinking seriously about sustainable development. Norman Myers (1989), a noted forest ecologist, penned an essay in *Foreign Policy* explicitly calling environment a new security issue. Jessica Tuchman Mathews (1989) opined in *Foreign Affairs* that resources were a new national security priority now that a redefinition was called for at the end of the Cold War. Michael Renner (1989) wrote a paper for the Worldwatch Institute that summarized the issue in terms of both economic and environmental dimensions. But much of this was reasonable speculation about what might happen and what ought to be done in case environmental matters spilled over into conflict or severely damaged societies even without overt conflict.

However, the military forces built up in the Cold War, equipped with tanks, missiles, nuclear weapons, fighter planes, and all the other equipment of war fighting, seemed completely useless in the face of environmental change. The fuel and resources used and the pollution and toxic waste produced by the military also suggested that this was a very inappropriate institution to deal with environmental problems, although its detailed knowledge of the environment and the military satellite and other surveillance systems might be useful (Prins 1993). However, if environmental changes did induce political elites to use force to try to deal with some of the problems of scarcity, or if war broke out as the dispossessed tried to seize control of resources they needed, then military action might once again be front and center of a new series of confrontations. This discussion of environmental security has been going on ever since.

All this was in the lead-up to the planned world leaders' summit in Rio de Janeiro in June 1992 on environment and development.

But prior to this some very old security priorities were to come to the fore once again when Saddam Hussein's forces invaded Kuwait in the summer of 1990 and the Americans assembled a coalition army in Saudi Arabia to evict the occupiers. As the Iraqi forces retreated early in 1991 they set numerous oil wells in Kuwait on fire. The images of blazing oil wells and the huge smoke cloud which drifted east and deposited soot on the ski slopes of the Himalayas once again linked war and the environment with powerful images of destruction. These images have subsequently become emblematic, recently gracing both the cover of Fred Kaplan's (2008) *Daydream Believers* on the Bush administration and the front of Geoff Dabelko's (2008) summary of the environmental security debate in *Environment* magazine.

Nonetheless the huge United Nations Conference on Environment and Development meetings, popularly known as "the Earth Summit," in Rio de Janeiro did happen in the first half of June 1992. Most world leaders gathered to finalize negotiations on a number of international agreements and in particular the Framework Convention on Climate Change. While the accomplishments were much more limited than many enthusiastic environmentalists might have hoped for (Chatterjee and Finger 1994), the civil society forum did facilitate numerous international dialogues and the formulation of the Earth Charter, which lays out many of the principles of sustainable living. Additional agreements on forests were drawn up as well as an ambitious program called Agenda 21, which some states followed up to involve communities in thinking and planning numerous local initiatives for more sustainable living. But little of all this is actually understood as a matter of security, despite Gro Harlem Brundtland's explicit invocation of the theme at Rio.

The Coming Anarchy?

Shortly after the Earth Summit, travel writer Robert Kaplan was traveling the world writing about the new security challenges now that the Cold War was over. He went to Africa and parts of the Middle East wondering about the environmental changes and political conflicts that he found. Going back to Malthus for inspiration he penned what has probably become the most influential essay on all this: "The Coming Anarchy," published as the cover story in the February 1994 issue of the *Atlantic Monthly*. More than any other contribution, this article focused attention in Washington, and subsequently elsewhere, on the debate about post-Cold War security concerns tied to environment. Kaplan's (1994: 58) prose is very dramatic:

> It is time to understand "the environment" for what it is: *the national-security issue of the early twenty-first century*. The political and strategic impact of surging populations, spreading disease, deforestation and soil erosion, water depletion, air pollution, and possibly, rising sea levels in critical overcrowded regions like the Nile Delta and Bangladesh – developments that will prompt mass migrations and, in turn, incite group conflicts – will be the core foreign-policy challenge from which most others will ultimately emanate, arousing the public and uniting assorted interests left over from the Cold War.

In many of the environmental security discussions, and in Kaplan's popular articulation of these themes in particular, there is nonetheless cause for alarm in the North. This is because of the potential that instability in the South may spill over into the zones of prosperity in the North; hence its formulation in the environmental security literature as a matter that "we" – security scholars and policy-makers in the North – ought to monitor.

In Kaplan's article and much of the rest of the literature in the 1990s, environmental degradation is a matter of Southern states and poor populations, not an issue directly concerning affluence (Dalby 2002). Environmental difficulties in the North are a matter for government regulation and of course technical innovation, but not a matter usually understood to have consequences in the South. Political instabilities might be expected in the South, especially in those areas not yet blessed by the political stability that supposedly comes from technological sophistication and democratic governance. Translated into Kaplan's (1994: 60) journalistic style:

> We are entering a bifurcated world. Part of the globe is inhabited by Hegel's and Fukuyama's Last Man, healthy, well fed, and pampered by technology. The other, larger, part is inhabited by

Hobbes's First Man, condemned to a life that is "poor, nasty, brutish, and short." Although both parts will be threatened by environmental stress, the Last Man will be able to master it; the First Man will not. The Last Man will adjust to the loss of underground water tables in the western United States. He will build dikes to save Cape Hatteras and the Chesapeake beaches from rising sea levels, even as the Maldive Islands, off the coast of India, sink into oblivion, and the shorelines of Egypt, Bangladesh, and Southeast Asia recede, driving tens of millions of people inland where there is no room for them, and thus sharpening ethnic divisions.

In the months following its publication this article was widely circulated in Washington and cited regularly in political discussion and congressional testimony. Combined with the contemporaneous debates about failed states (Esty et al. 1998), their potential for spillover effects in matters of international security (Esty 1999), and Vice President Al Gore's concerns with global environmental matters and climate change in particular, the theme of environmental security was clearly on the policy agenda in Washington.

The environmental security discussion has been re-invigorated a decade later by renewed attention to matters of climate change and global security, especially since the United Nations Security Council debated the matter in April 2007. Europeans in particular have paid attention to it as part of their discussions of the policies needed to de-carbonize the European economy as a contribution to tackling climate change. The current focus on climate change has made this whole debate on environmental security current once again, but now poses its concerns at the largest of scales. Scholarly research in the 1990s made it clear that many of the more alarmist claims about war between the North and South over environmental matters were unfounded (Homer-Dixon 1999). Few plausible scenarios existed in which states would go to war over ozone depletion, or over climate change or the extinction of whales. It turned out that water wars were also unlikely (Lonergan 2001), not least because with a few exceptions, like the case of the Nile river in Africa, militarily powerful states don't exist downstream from states likely to stop the flow of water (Gleditsch et al. 2006). Investigations suggested in many cases that cooperation is encouraged in a crisis rather than conflict; the opposite case that environmental cooperation might lead to peace or at least prevent the outbreak of hostilities was made plausibly too (Conca and Dabelko 2002). Conservation areas and national parks usefully contribute to peacemaking on disputed frontiers in many places, not least by encouraging cooperation across boundaries (Ali 2007), but much of this literature was ignored in the newfound concern with climate change and the assumptions that disasters would lead to international conflict (Floyd 2008). Updated to deal with climate change, the same arguments apply, and there is little in the scholarly literature to suggest that war over climate change is a realistic danger (Salehyan 2008).

Global Environmental Change and Climate Disaster?

While the IPCC continued its work through the 1990s and into the new millennium, compiling and assessing the rapidly accumulating scientific work on climate change, the negotiations about the practical arrangements for dealing with climate change under the convention proceeded very slowly and acrimoniously; not least because of opposition to any such arrangements on the part of the oil and coal industries in many places, and in the United States in particular. Nonetheless the Kyoto protocol was agreed and the European Union in particular began steps toward de-carbonizing its economy to reduce greenhouse gas emissions. Developing states were once again suspicious of Northern agendas; the initial Kyoto process involved them joining in later, once clear progress on reductions and on providing alternative technologies was demonstrated.

But when George W. Bush was appointed president by the U.S. Supreme Court late in 2000, it was clear that once again American politicians with important connections into the oil industry were back in the White House and that environmental matters would probably get low priority. The Kyoto protocol appeared dead given the refusal of the administration to ratify it. Nonetheless with Russian accession some years later it did eventually come into force, on 16 February 2005, although by then it was clear that many states were not going to meet their commitments. In the meantime the events of 9/11 and the subsequent launch of the "global war on terror" moved environmental matters off the agenda for a few years; military definitions of security once again gained prominence temporarily.

But concerns with climate change did not go away. The evidence of continued change in temperatures, melting ice caps and glaciers, changing migration patterns, early arrival of spring in many parts of the Northern hemisphere, has now become overwhelming and so climate change is once again on everyone's mind. The security implications of increased storms and the possible disruptions of major parts of modern societies were unavoidable in the aftermath of Hurricane Katrina and the flooding of New Orleans. In April 2007 the United Nations Security Council debated the issue of climate change, suggesting to many commentators that there was finally a dawning recognition that major disruptions are actually coming. Movies, technical reports, a reluctant admission on the part of the Bush administration that climate change needed to be addressed, an abrupt rhetorical about-face by the Conservative federal government in Canada, all suggested that climate change could no longer be denied. Carbon fuels bring with them a very inconvenient truth, to borrow Nobel prize-winner Al Gore's apt wording; they literally do change the air we breathe, with potentially huge consequences for future generations.

The year 2007 also witnessed the publication of numerous technical reports on climate change, not least the fourth assessment by the IPCC, whose results were unequivocal about the human factors in changing the climate. Numerous policy papers and even Congressional action requiring a National Intelligence Estimate in 2008 based on the IPCC scenarios show that this is now once again linked explicitly to discussions of security. These reports will be discussed in more detail in chapter 4, but it is worth emphasizing here that the United Nations Environment Program *GEO4 Global Environmental Outlook* published in 2007 also raised the alarm about climate change, as did the *United Nations Development Report 2007–2008* (UNDP 2007), which explicitly focused on possible conflict as a result of climate change. Much commentary also followed on from the United Kingdom government (UK Treasury Department 2007)

Stern review of *The Economics of Climate Change*, a noteworthy publication because it firmly suggested that it would be cheaper to take preventive action now, rather than have to pay to deal with the much worse consequences of climate change later, and also for its blunt statement that the market had failed to send any appropriate signals to deal with the crisis.

While many of these reports are careful and conservative in their estimations of future events, there is a sense that major changes are afoot. The earlier discussions of the limits to growth in the 1970s, with their very long-term predictions about change, may actually be beginning to happen now (Graham Turner 2008). As 2008 began, a dramatic spike in oil prices and in food prices suggested that some of the Malthusian discussions about limits might also be relevant. The irony of switching from food crops to bio-fuel crops, which are allegedly part of the solution to climate change, causing great suffering among the poorest of the world's population – precisely those who do not have the cars that cause greenhouse gas emissions – is not lost on at least some commentators. But there have been dramatic spikes in oil prices in the past, not least in the 1970s due to political upheavals in the Middle East; food crises too are tied into the complex functioning of international markets.

One of the most worrying warnings in the scientific literature on climate change is the simple matter that environmental systems don't necessarily respond in straightforward and predictable ways. There is every reason to expect rapid responses by the world's climate system to the current disruptions (Schneider 2004). Pushed to extremes they may suddenly change in a "non-linear" fashion, as when a forest burns and suddenly changes from a collection of mature trees to a scorched landscape in which new growth starts the cycle all over again. Other changes, in climate or moisture availability, the introduction of diseases or new animals, may mean that the new growth doesn't produce a similar forest to the old one at all. When human systems are involved, further complications are introduced that make ecological predictions even more difficult (Gunderson and Holling 2002). On the largest scale of the biosphere as a whole such matters are even harder to predict, although the sophisticated climate models are becoming capable of predicting past climates at least.

One non-linearity that has gained much attention is the possibility of abrupt climate change as a result of climate change switching off the so-called "thermohaline conveyor" ocean current system (Alley 2004). Sometimes known simply as the Gulf Stream, the most important part of this current flows from the Gulf of Mexico across the Atlantic, past the British Isles and Iceland. In doing so it keeps the climate of Northern Europe much warmer than other places of similar latitude. Once these waters flow close to the Arctic they sink into the ocean depths and flow back round the planet in a complex pattern that effectively keeps all the world's oceans moving, and the climate pattern relatively predictable in many places. What makes the waters of the Atlantic part of the conveyor belt, which sinks as it gets into high latitudes, is their relative temperature and salinity. Current conditions make these waters marginally more dense than other Arctic waters, so they sink. Minor changes, either increased temperature or decreased salinity due to increased freshwater runoff from Greenland and elsewhere in the Northern hemisphere, might cause the conveyor to slow or even stop, inducing numerous climate changes in various parts of the world (Vellinga and Wood 2002).

This scenario was the basis of the 2004 Hollywood disaster movie *The Day After Tomorrow*, and while the climate system just doesn't react as quickly as the movie's scriptwriters suggest, clearly the potential for disruption is huge. While recent scientific estimates have suggested that the possibilities of the conveyor slowing dramatically in the foreseeable future are fairly small, nonetheless, because of the dramatic repercussions should it happen, it's the kind of non-linearity that worries security thinkers. A scenario planning exercise by some Pentagon consultants in 2003 investigated precisely this event and concluded that the world would be hard pressed to cope with the disruptions set in motion (Schwartz and Randall 2003). Looking at a situation where the average temperature drops 5 or 6 degrees in Europe and North America, increases by similar amounts in Southern Africa, Latin America, and Australia, where droughts reduce agricultural output in the North Eastern United States and much of Europe while storms are more intense in many places, Schwartz and Randall suggest that such changes might lead to conflict and possibly war as a result of "1) Food shortages due to decreases in net global agricultural production; 2) Decreased availability and quality of fresh water in key regions due to shifted precipitation patterns, causing more frequent floods and droughts; 3) Disrupted access to energy supplies due to extensive sea ice and storminess" (2003: 2). In turn this might set in motion all sorts of migrations and destabilize regimes unable to feed their populations. War in some form or other is not unlikely in these circumstances.

Although recent research suggests that sudden disruptions of the Atlantic conveyor system are unlikely (IPCC 2007), concern remains that surprises await us. Most worrying is the fact that rapid non-linear ecological events are a matter of geological record and there is no reason to expect that current anthropogenic changes will not lead to sudden, unexpected results. In the worst-case scenario, might they lead to civilizational collapse, or at least to dramatic political and economic changes? These kinds of questions have sent scholars and policy-makers to the history books looking for linkages between past human events and their ecological contexts. Is there historical evidence that supports contentions about dramatic social and economic disruptions as a result of environmental change? The answer is yes, but in many cases the causal connections are not so clear, the historical record is ambiguous, and the precise nature of environmental change hard to quantify. There is much we simply don't know, and while the scientific reconstruction of past environments will no doubt reveal many new dimensions of our history, where written records don't exist much of the human response has to be interpolated from the pieces we do know. Worse still are the difficulties that come with efforts to draw historical parallels to present circumstances. This is so because, as much of the rest of this book will show, our current circumstances are now much more a matter of our own making than was the case in previous periods of history.

Environmental Change or Collapse?

On the long timescale, one going back over hundreds of thousands of years, it's clear that ice ages and the interglacial periods in between have profoundly shaped human history. Fifteen thousand years ago, where my university now stands was under a large ice sheet. In the unlikely event that there were any humans here then, they left no evidence to be found. Humans moved across the earth as the last ice age retreated, and on the big scale this is perhaps the most important point to remember. Civilization is a very new phenomenon in geological terms and trivial in duration in comparison to ice ages and geological cycles that stretch back over hundreds of thousands of years. Brian Fagan's (1999, 2004) popular books on climate outline some of the previous episodes in history when climate has apparently caused changes in human affairs, but earlier systematic work by scholars, and in particular H. H. Lamb (1995), allows some informed summary of earlier episodes of change where clearly populations suffered when food supplies ran out because of climate changes. More recent attempts to link the emerging data on climate change in the past with warfare events has suggested that, especially in the case of Chinese history, warfare is related to climate change, and more specifically with the carrying capacity of land that fluctuates depending on climate (Zhang et al. 2007).

Some of environmental history is about periodic fluctuations in climate, and here the El Niño phenomenon gets pride of place. Disasters and disruptions make for exciting reading and the search for historical explanation in the natural world suggests that there are lessons we might learn. But as Fagan (1999) explains at the beginning of his *Floods, Famines and Emperors*, one of the most useful of all is that we can prepare for floods and famines, and unlike many earlier societies, we have a technology of climate modeling and weather forecasting that allows us to avoid the worst effects of the weather, precisely because we can make reasonable forecasts of what's coming and, if we pay attention, plan accordingly. Likewise our transportation technology allows us to move food supplies to tackle famines in ways that previous societies haven't been able or, more recently, willing to do. Caution is needed in drawing from earlier periods of history to tackle our current situation, but Zhang et al.'s (2007) warning that a substantial part of humanity will remain dependent on small-scale agriculture for the foreseeable future, and hence directly vulnerable to climate change, remains key to all the discussions of rural vulnerability in Africa and elsewhere in the developing world (Barnett and Adger 2007).

Jared Diamond's (2005) *Collapse* raises the really big question of the complete eradication of societies and even civilizations, and the ecological bases of these events. Some cases lack a detailed historical record and speculation is needed to fill in the gaps. Others can be worked through in detail, and Diamond's analysis of South Pacific islands in particular, with their limited ecological possibilities, is especially convincing on the limits that were possible for local populations however ingenious they might be. Diamond's book raises the question of the complete collapse of the contemporary human civilization, and whether the extraordinary exploitation of the biosphere that we have recently set in motion is in fact a prelude to exhaustion and collapse. His suggestion in the end that we have one large advantage that the other cases in his study didn't is intriguing, but not necessarily reassuring, because elites caught up with immediate rivalries and other preoccupations may be uninterested in thinking about innovation or the long term (McNeill 2005). Diamond's argument is that we know what happened in the earlier cases, at least in broad outline, and that by the careful application of historical and scientific reasoning we can infer and deduce the missing pieces of previous events. Earlier societies probably didn't have a clear idea of any of the other cases, in which case we ought to be able to anticipate looming crises and change behavior in time to avert catastrophe. But the question as to whether historical analogies from earlier cases are either accurate or appropriate in present circumstances isn't an easy one to answer, given the scale of contemporary globalization and the sheer speed of technological innovation in the last couple of centuries.

Posing the question of whether our society is facing collapse so bluntly, in other words as an existential threat, does suggest that environmental matters ought to be thought of in terms of security. Environmental security is, in this sense, about the conditions that make civilization possible, and these need to be secured as the precondition for all other human activities; therefore if ever there is a security issue this is surely it! But specifying precisely what those conditions are isn't so easy, given the adaptability of human societies and the possibilities for additional technological innovation in the immediate future. Neither is it so easy unless very different policy tools and institutions are involved in thinking about global security in a biosphere that we are actively changing (Worldwatch Institute 2005). Many of the hazards that may turn into disasters aren't deliberate attempts on the part of a polity to inflict damage on another. However, the human security agenda, and in particular the UNDP Report version formulated in 1994, emphasizes that human security is frequently about amorphous threats that are unintentional and global. In Gwyn Prins' (1993) terms these are "threats without enemies."

But is this formulation really about things that are usefully understood in terms of "security"? Security has become a key term in political discourse and policy legitimation in the years since the Second World War; it remains a highly contested term, which bears examination in some detail if the multiple meanings it has are to be brought to bear on environmental matters. They are linked in numerous ways; being clear about how they have been linked is key to understanding how these terms are now invoked in the discussion of climate change in particular and global environmental change more generally. This is the topic for chapter 2.

2
Securing Precisely What? Global, Environmental, and Human Security

In the aftermath of the Second World War, with the arrival of the Cold War, atomic bombs, and then the more powerful hydrogen ones, matters of war, peace, and international relations took on new, complicated technological dimensions. Indeed, precisely because of the interconnections between technology, international relations, and the widespread diplomatic responsibilities the United States had suddenly acquired in 1945, an overarching conception for policy formulation that would clarify priorities in the new circumstances was needed in Washington (Yergin 1977). This came initially in discussions of a "national security interest" wherein military, diplomatic, and economic dimensions of statecraft were connected into a policy agenda. With war rendered illegal under the United Nations charter, and only defense being allowed, the language of "national security" permeated many aspects of politics where international relations and violence were part of the policy considerations.

The dangers of war between the superpowers, and the nuclear fallout that would result if large numbers of nuclear weapons were used, suggested that there were global dimensions to all this that also needed attention. The consequences of war in the 1940s had reverberated round the world, and the possibility of nuclear warfare made it clear that this would involve people in many places even if their states were not combatants. Indeed much of the rationale for the existence of the United Nations was about the maintenance of international peace and security precisely because of the danger that small instabilities and conflicts might escalate to engulf the superpowers, and hence lead to a war that would be global in scope if nuclear weapons were used to tackle military and civilian targets. Hence these matters of common concern to all humanity came to be understood as matters of global security.

Global Security and Nuclear War

The link to environmental matters came fairly early on in all this. Fallout from nuclear tests in the atmosphere in the 1950s traveled round the world, getting into children's teeth in all societies. The health implications for people round the world added to arguments for nuclear disarmament in general, but more specifically to calls for an international agreement to stop nuclear testing in the atmosphere. While the atmospheric nuclear test ban treaty of the 1960s is frequently understood as an arms control treaty, Marvin Soroos (1997) argues that in fact, given the focus on reducing the dangers of radioactive fallout from the tests to human populations, it was an international environmental treaty. Thus in some crucial senses the partial test ban treaty, which effectively ended nuclear bomb tests in the atmosphere in the early 1960s, was the first global atmospheric environmental treaty, even if it isn't frequently remembered as such. This might well mean that this agreement, understood as an environmental treaty, was in fact the first explicitly dealing with environmental security as we later came to understand it.

Especially worrying to some atmospheric scientists was the prospect of a nuclear war disrupting the ozone layer in the upper atmosphere; nuclear tests had suggested that high-altitude blasts in particular might at least temporarily compromise the crucial function of the layer in preventing harmful ultraviolet radiation reaching the surface of the earth. It turned out in the 1980s that chlorofluorocarbons did the same thing, requiring a global ban on their production to ensure that in the long run the ozone layer will recover (Makhijani and Gurney 1995).

While the Cold War confrontation dominated international politics through the years leading up to 1989, the predominant focus of strategic and security thinking was on matters of the dangers of nuclear war and the confrontation between the superpowers and their alliance systems. Questions of political order were related to the dangers of external subversion from the other bloc, and to matters of development in what was usually simply referred to as the Third World. The struggle for influence, and to direct the course of development, there led to proxy wars and political violence in many places.

Superpower rivalries became especially fraught in the first Reagan presidency in the early 1980s, when the rearmament of the United States took place along with discussions of nuclear war fighting strategies. At the height of this second Cold War confrontation a Korean airliner was shot down over Sakhalin Island in September 1983 by the Soviet air force and fears of war were immediately raised.

Shortly after this, scientists made headlines with an alarming study that predicted dramatic short-term climate disruptions in the aftermath of a major nuclear war (Turco et al. 1983). It became clear that not only would the world face the immediate catastrophe of nuclear bombs destroying many cities and killing hundreds of millions of people in a matter of hours, but that in addition to the economic disruptions and the legacy of illness from radioactive fallout, the global climate too would be disrupted. In the more worrying scenarios this suggested that for years afterwards the Northern hemisphere at least would be shaded by the dust and smoke lofted into the stratosphere by the explosions and subsequent fires. In these circumstances agriculture would be dramatically reduced and in many places impossible. Other ecological disruptions would also occur with unpredictable results. The phrase "nuclear winter" entered popular vocabulary.

The nuclear winter argument suggested that the ecological consequences of a nuclear war would dwarf the immediate war damage; there would be no winners in such circumstances (Sagan and Turco 1990). The survival of human civilization itself was in peril and thus the impetus to step back from the brink of nuclear confrontation was compelling. Clearly all humans were insecure in the face of nuclear warfare, not only because of the war itself but also because of the long-term ecological disruptions. Security provided by mutually assured destruction threatened insecurity for all in the strange logic of the Cold War. Whatever claims nuclear strategists might make about a strategy of victory, a matter of targeting an opponent so that damage was limited and the war won, paled in comparison to the threats to the integrity of the biosphere. Ecological thinking added a powerful additional element to the arguments about superpower mutually assured destruction being a very stupid way to run a small planet.

In retrospect it seems clear that the nuclear winter discussion had more impact in Moscow than in Washington and was part of the reason that the Soviet Union changed its course in the late 1980s toward new thinking and a security strategy that was much less confrontational. Dramatic arms cuts and the withdrawal of destabilizing weapons systems came along with the policies of perestroika. The reactor meltdown at Chernobyl in 1986 likewise made even contemplating warfare in Europe, where hundreds of reactors dotted the landscape, unthinkable to the Gorbachev administration. A military solution to a confrontation with the United States was simply too dangerous to contemplate, and so a strategy of political management to ensure hostilities did not happen was needed (MccGwire 1991). New thinking about security was in part a response to a recognition of the ecological vulnerabilities of the new technological circumstances of humanity. Subsequently when the Soviet Union collapsed in 1991 these crucial insights were swept aside in a triumphal narrative in Washington. The neo-conservative forces celebrated victory, claimed that the Reagan military buildup had driven the Soviet Union into bankruptcy; the end of history was apparently at hand, and military coercion supposedly had worked.

But while this interpretation of events has subsequently been used much more recently as part of the rationale legitimating the Bush doctrine (Fred Kaplan 2008), many other thinkers have looked to other formulations of security in the aftermath of the Cold War. A key theme has been to extend the remit of security, to cover new threats including unintentional changes that may disrupt and endanger societies and states, to extend the agencies that are involved in providing security, and to recognize that people in numerous places are insecure, so states alone cannot be the objects that are secured (Rothschild 1995). Indeed the more challenging thinking has suggested that, given the violence done by states, the more appropriate referent of security should be people, not states. In some cases this suggests clearly that states are the cause of insecurity, a reversal of much of the Cold War thinking that presumed that states are the providers of security for their populations, all of which emphasizes the crucial importance of who invokes the language of threats and insecurity in this whole discussion (Fierke 2007).

This insight suggests that security isn't a matter of objective circumstances, of inevitable threats, and of the necessity for military preparations to tackle the external dangers. In the aftermath of the Cold War, thinking about the expansion of the remit of security and its linkage to all sorts of phenomena has lead to a widespread understanding that security is very much a political matter (Buzan et al. 1998). How dangers are specified, and extraordinary measures set in motion to deal with the danger so specified, are frequently now understood in terms of securitization. This is an active process of the discursive specification of danger that involves both the enunciation of a threat by an authority figure and an audience that concurs up to a point at least with the specification of the danger (M. C. Williams 2003). Then measures can be taken, troops drafted, weapons and plans to use them drawn up, emergency rule instituted, and the apparatus of national security set in motion.

In the last couple of decades numerous threats of biological and environmental hazards have been crafted and become part of both popular culture and state security discourse, especially since 9/11. This is not to deny that some fears are justified; diseases do kill people. But how these are treated by social actors matters. If diseases are a security threat, different agencies respond than if they are seen solely as a matter for doctors and public health officials. If those diseases are used as an excuse for other forms of social action then, while they are threatening, they are so in a variety of different ways. The complicated debate about HIV/AIDS suggests clearly that there are numerous ways of dealing with the syndrome; punitive measures and policing on the one hand, medical interventions and therapy on the other. Fears are part of social life, but for the purposes of the analysis in this book the important thing is to understand that: "Fears are the products of particular historical intersections and political, cultural and technological conjunctures." (Hartmann et al. 2005: 3). There are also important overlaps and interconnections between the larger social imaginary in which fears are constructed and the social institutions that are called upon to police and control the threats.

Security in the contemporary age is also about technical matters, whether it is screening people at airports, inoculating populations against influenza, or planning to deal with incoming missiles. The environment is no exception to this pattern, and as this book makes clear, quite how environment is specified as a threat in need of security is a key point. But which institutions are called upon likewise is important. Much of the discussion is about development, or rather the dangers of the lack of development, which supposedly render marginal populations vulnerable. Should violence among the poor spread to the affluent parts of the planet then that insecurity becomes part of the security agenda for conventional military and state forces. But should the byproducts of that affluence render the poor and marginal insecure then a very different geopolitics is at work, one that is partly covered in the debate about sustainable development, and one which is now unavoidable because of climate change. In short, security in these terms isn't about states and their rivalries, it's about people facing numerous insecurities, from many of which states either can't or won't protect populations. It's about what has come to be called human security.

Human Security and Environment

In 1994 the UNDP encapsulated the new, broader security agenda in the post-Cold War world in a discussion of human security. The UNDP authors argued that "The concept of security has for too long been interpreted narrowly: as security of territory from external aggression, or as protection of national interest in foreign policy or as global security from the threat of a nuclear holocaust. It has been related more to nation-states than to people" (UNDP 1994: 22). This suggestion challenged the implicit assumption in most security studies that states were the most important entity and that war is the primary danger facing humanity. Once the nuclear standoff between the superpowers was over, as it clearly was by the early 1990s, other matters could intrude on discussions of survival, state policy, and long-term security planning.

The concept of human security had, they asserted, at least four essential characteristics. First, it is a universal concern relevant to people everywhere. Second, the components of security are interdependent. Third, human security is easier to ensure through early prevention. Fourth, and perhaps the crucial innovation in this formulation, is the shift of the referent object of security from states to people. More explicitly, this formulation defines human security as "first, safety from such chronic threats as hunger, disease and repression. And second, it means protection from sudden and hurtful disruptions in the patterns of daily life – whether in homes, in jobs or in communities. Such threats can exist at all levels of national income and development" (UNDP 1994: 23).

The argument suggests that the concept of security must change away from Cold War and realist preoccupations with territorial security to focus on people's security, and from armaments toward a reformulation in terms of sustainable human development. Demilitarization is obviously part of this agenda, but human welfare broadly conceived is the overall thrust of the concept. As such there are numerous threats to human security, although specific threats are likely to be locale dependent. Nonetheless, according to the UNDP threats to human security come under seven general categories: economic, food, health, environmental, personal, community, and political.

While many of the UNDP list of threats to human security are local, global ones are said to include at least six categories, caused more by the actions of millions of people than by the deliberate aggression of specific states. As such they would thus not be considered security threats under most narrow formulations of security studies. These six are (1) unchecked population growth, (2) disparities in economic opportunities, (3) excessive international migration, (4) environmental degradation, (5) drug production and trafficking, and (6) international terrorism (UNDP 1994: 34). These categories and the formulation of human security underlay a growing number of assessments of the state of world politics in the 1990s and attempts to encapsulate political agendas for reform of the international system (Commission on Global Governance 1995; Independent Commission on Population and Quality of Life 1996). While these themes were temporarily removed from the international agenda in the immediate aftermath of the events of September 11, 2001, they reappeared later in the decade as part of the United Nations deliberations about security and the secretary-general's panel on high-level threats (United Nations High-Level Panel on Threats, Challenges and Change 2004), and have been recently re-addressed in part as a result of the rejuvenated discussion of climate change and its implications.

More specifically, when the UNDP authors turned their attention to environmental matters they looked to national concerns, or environmental threats within countries, including in developing countries where clean water supply, loss of forests, and desertification are noted as particular problems (UNDP 1994: 28–30). In industrial states, air pollution in big cities and the loss of forests and agricultural land due to pollution are noted. Salinization of farmland and severe floods and droughts due to land use changes are noted, as is the fact that people moved onto marginal land are more vulnerable to natural hazards. Cyclones, which hit Bangladesh regularly, get a special mention. The discussion of global environmental threats includes acid rain in Europe, chlorofluorocarbons and the ozone layer depletion, greenhouse gas emissions, loss of biological diversity, accelerated coastal marine pollution, and declines in fish catches as well as coral reef loss and the fragmentation of valuable habitats (UNDP 1994: 35–6).

But while this comprehensive agenda of policy aspirations and its attempt to re-interpret the priorities for international politics covered many of the issues discussed in the 1990s, it offered neither obvious priorities for policy nor an effective analytical lens through which research could be conducted on the parameters of human insecurity. Policy aspiration and academic analysis merge here frequently in various ways, but the sheer breadth that related environmental matters to human insecurities in numerous ways precluded any clear research agenda or policy focus. Nonetheless the link between human security and environment had been clearly made in this document, and it was to influence many researchers subsequently. The fact that this formulation of human security came from the UNDP with its focus on development emphasizes the discussion of the vulnerability of the most marginal and the poor; those for whom development supposedly promises a better life.

Globalization and Environmental Insecurity

It was precisely these poor and marginal peoples who were the object of some of the early 1990s literature that formulated matters in Malthusian terms of population growth as the primary threat to security. The contrast between the Malthusian approach – Robert Kaplan's 1994 article on "The Coming Anarchy" highlighted this theme – which effectively blames the poor as the authors of their own misfortune, and the more sophisticated thinking that starts with simple empirical questions concerning the causes of their insecurity, emphasizes the importance of the politics implicit in formulations of human security. Michael Thompson's (1998) scathing critique of Malthusian environmental security thinking showed that much of the Malthusian approach is premised on a false, ethnocentric assumption of the "ignorant fecund peasant" as the root of Third World troubles. The "ignorant fecund peasant" model of overpopulation leading to environmental crisis, which is so popular with Northern environmentalists, is inaccurate, not least because of the gross overgeneralizations about peasant behavior, but more importantly because of the overlooked intricacies of rural political ecologies, as well as global trade interconnections.

In stark contrast to simplistic neo-Malthusian understandings, Michael Renner (1996) of the Worldwatch Institute in Washington used the United Nations' concept of human security to investigate the global connections between environmental problems and social conflict. Pointing to the growing inequities in the global political economy, he suggested that these are related in various ways to both degradation and conflict. Renner (1996: 17) asserted that "It is becoming clear that humanity is facing a triple security crisis: societies everywhere have to contend with the effects of environmental decline, the repercussions of social inequities and stress, and the dangers arising out of an unchecked arms proliferation that is a direct legacy of the Cold War period." Human security worries, he continued, "are now magnified by the unprecedented scale of environmental degradation, by the presence of immense poverty in the midst of extraordinary wealth, and by the fact that social, economic, and environmental challenges are no longer limited to particular communities and nations" (Renner 1996: 18). Political violence is often widespread in places where war is not officially occurring.

But political fragmentation, fueled by the proliferation of weapons, is only one half of the story of human insecurity (Kaldor 2007). The other half is the accelerating processes of globalization that are interconnecting the world's economies and cultures in ways that often operate to undercut traditional economies and challenge the sustainability of agricultural and survival practices. Wars in the South are now frequently about who will control the revenue from the extraction of resources for sale on the global market; a form of "shadow globalization" that has gradually come to be recognized as a matter of insecurity due to the connections of the global economy rather than any intrinsic local scarcities (Jung 2003). The processes of accelerating globalization explain much more than the geopolitically inadequate formulations of Malthusianism, which continue to assume that difficulties are driven by local, autonomous processes of overpopulation (Peluso and Watts 2001).

Renner's (1996) argument, picking up on contemporaneous critiques of the operation of the global economy and matters of international debt and development (Mander and Goldsmith 1996), suggested the forces setting populations in motion were a crucial dimension of human insecurity. Looking to the global interconnections puts human security into the circuits of the global economy, and reminds readers that famines are about poverty much more than about food shortages. The historical patterns of commodification, overexploitation, and domestication of resources in the expansion of commercial economies are not new, as will be discussed in chapter 3. Neither are the population disruptions and displacements that often result. These displaced people may in turn damage marginal lands unsuited to agriculture, or swell the ranks of the poor in urban shanty towns and become a matter of concern to environmentalists (Homer-Dixon 1999). The interconnections between globalization and environmental degradation are crucial to Renner's (1996) argument, but the processes in motion are also those carried out by political and military elites. Modernization is about state-making. The enclosures and displacement of rural populations that are part of the state-backed and state-enforced expansion of commercial agriculture cause the displacement of many "environmental refugees" (Gadgil and Guha 1995).

On the largest scale, these people become the object of Malthusian security narratives on the crises of migration, and invoke alarm as migrants apparently threaten the integrity of the nation to which they flee. Renner's (1996) point is that rural land reform and the construction of less unequal landholding arrangements are often the key to improving environmental conditions and other facets of life in rural areas. But such initiatives may run directly up against elites whose power and wealth rest on the unequal landholdings, and whose businesses dominate the expanding commercial sector of the agricultural economy of developing states. As Colin Kahl's (2006) research has subsequently illustrated, where this is engaged in agricultural production for export, sometimes partly as a result of internationally imposed economic conditionalities and structural adjustment policies, the links between globalization and peasant struggles are especially direct. Getting the geography of these insecurities clear is an important part of contextualizing both human security and the debate about the relationships of environment and conflict. This is especially so when alarmist suggestions are made that environmental factors may cause wars in the near future, or at least are serious enough matters to invoke the attention of the security apparatuses of states and of politicians anxious to use fears of many threats for their own purposes. This point raises an additional crucial matter: the question of who specifies issues as being important enough to justify the invocation of the language of security. Security is a very complicated term, and one that is frequently invoked in a crisis. Its meanings and uses are neither simple, nor given in any particular set of circumstances.

Securitization

The term "security" is highly contested in both scholarly and political usage (Dalby 1997, 2002; Steve Smith 2005). Linking it to environment complicates matters even further, and there is no commonly agreed understanding of how these terms might be linked or even whether they should be. Nonetheless this is repeatedly done when alarms about environment are turned into questions of supposedly high political priority (Hartmann et al. 2005). The politics of security thus is a crucial part of any analysis that links environment with discussions of security. Who invokes an emergency situation requiring a security response is part of the matter; but so too is the specification of who or what is endangered in these circumstances. All this is what is meant by "securitization"; the active processes of invoking security and setting in motion policies and actions on the basis of presenting matters as threatening. This has been done repeatedly in the last few decades in discussions of environment, but not usually with much success.

Securitization is a mode of analysis most closely associated with the so-called Copenhagen school of security studies that drew on the critical literature in linguistics and elsewhere to point out that security was in part a speech act, a performance of the invocation of danger as requiring extraordinary action (Buzan et al. 1998) Security is in this mode of thinking, not a simple term nor an objectively agreed upon condition. When used in discussions of politics it is a powerful word, invoking a desired state as well as a threat to that state that requires protective measures. When something is securitized, made the referent object of those measures and constructed in policy discourse as in need of being secured, it then becomes the focus of state actions. Resources are mobilized, troops may be deployed, surveillance undertaken. Emergency measures may be called for that necessitate the suspension of normal rules of law, and the granting of additional powers to police or military agencies. In the process, who and what precisely is secured becomes important.

Claims by rulers to be acting in the common good are frequent in these circumstances, but frequently such claims turn out to be misleading at best, and at worst a strategy to stay in power by using violence and fear as tools of rule (Fierke 2007). Insofar as environment is portrayed as a threat, and international stability is upset by migration or conflicts over resources, these long-established patterns may recur. But they may not do much to deal with either the threats or their causes. As much of the rest of this book suggests, this is in part because the attribution of the source of danger to external causes, rather than construing it as a consequence of metropolitan patterns of consumption, turns out not to deal with many environmental matters very effectively.

Neither are all invocations of danger necessarily effective (Fierke 2007). Politicians who invoke threats are not always successful at convincing their audiences either of the imminent dangers or of their capabilities for dealing with the threats they portray. Thus security is a political act of mobilization of support for actions, which requires that the audience accept the definition of danger and agrees at least tacitly to the use of security measures to deal with the situation. If the narrative is not convincing, or the costs of dealing with the danger seem to outweigh the potential threat, then securitization is unlikely to be successful. If the tools to deal with the task are not available then attempting to securitize an issue is likewise unlikely to be effective, unless the task and the tools are redefined so that the threat is amenable to those tools. Finally, there is of course the logical possibility that the audience does buy the argument and agrees to the mobilization of resources, but the result is an ineffective policy response regardless of the success of the initial securitization.

Michael C. Williams (2003) adds an important supplement to the Copenhagen school's approach, emphasizing that more than speech acts are involved in the communication processes related to security. In the aftermath of the events of September 11 he emphasizes the importance of televisual images as key to political communication. While George W. Bush may have followed up Tony Blair's bellicose formulation of the events in terms of a "war on terror," the images of the collapsing towers, played over and over again on television, were the defining ones of the times. Likewise the media coverage of Hurricane Katrina, with the numerous images of floods and military interventions, has left indelible images of destruction as its semiotic legacy; so too in the case of the environmental security debate the images of blazing oil wells in Kuwait provide images that recur repeatedly. But the satellite images of Hurricane Katrina with the eye of the storm over the Southern United States is also a symbol of this event. When linked to the smoke emitted from industrial smokestacks, as in the powerful graphic that accompanies Al Gore's lecture and movie *An Inconvenient Truth*, these images convey powerful senses of endangerment too, complementing the oil-well fires as defining images of the theme.

As Michael C. Williams (2003) notes, it is precisely when extreme danger is invoked in political discourse that security is most efficacious. An existential threat, one in which survival is in question, most obviously requires extreme measures. The Cold War, where the Soviet

Threat was portrayed as an existential threat to Western society and to Christianity itself, clearly justified spy agencies, military mobilization, nuclear weapons, missiles, and the whole panoply of Cold War political and economic institutions. In the face of global environmental change the existence of the necessary ecological conditions for civilization can be portrayed as an existential issue for contemporary society. Hence linking security and environment makes sense in this framework insofar as the conditions that allow for modern societies to function might be endangered by environmental changes. While that would seem to be such an obvious argument as to preclude further comment, as later chapters in this book will show there is a long, complicated history of arguments about the relationship of environment and civilization, which makes such securitizations much more difficult to effectively apply than might initially appear to be the case. But this crucial insight does tie the discussion rhetorically, at least, to the popular discussions about disaster, collapse, and the appropriate policy responses in such circumstances.

Securitizing Environment

Securitization is hence especially relevant to the debate about environmental security where many of these arguments have played out a number of times, and are frequently forgotten in the contemporary concerns with climate change (Floyd 2008). Gwyn Prins posed the question of the appropriateness of the military as an agent of environmental security very clearly in choosing the title *Top Guns and Toxic Whales* for his documentary film and his coauthored companion book on the subject in the early 1990s (Prins and Stamp 1991). The Top Guns in his title are the fighter pilots flying hugely sophisticated stealth bombers that supposedly provide national security for modern states by attacking any potential invaders. But they are powerless to do anything about the poisoning of the seas, which endangers whales. In the late 1980s, prior to Prins making his documentary, some whales ingested so much polluted seafood and concentrated the contaminants in their flesh to such a degree that they were considered toxic waste when they died. Someone has to deal with the whale carcasses washing up on the beach, but air force pilots and their hugely expensive machines aren't going to be much help. The military is not apparently the kind of agency that is needed to deal with environmental threats to wellbeing.

Daniel Deudney (1990, 1999a, 1999b) explored this line of argument further in his writings and raised the additional point that invoking national security may actually be counterproductive, given that international cooperation is what is needed to deal with most environmental difficulties. Invoking nationalism and thinking in military terms only make matters worse by specifying external threats rather than common dangers. The threats from traditional military concerns of security are different from environmental ones and hence traditional ways of thinking are inappropriate. Military threats are usually from states; they are violent and direct intentional acts; environmental threats tend to be diffuse, indirect, and international, originating both inside and outside the state concerned. Military threats are occasional and unusual events; environmental degradation is a long-term process usually derived accidentally from routine economic activities. As we have seen in chapter 1, in Robert Kaplan's (1994) representation of the poor states of the South as a threat to the North, such geopolitical reasoning is more likely to lead to policies that try to limit migration or use violence to control change than it is to getting at the root causes of poverty and the global disruptions of natural systems.

If, as Deudney concluded, you add into the whole argument the point that wars are unlikely to be caused by environmental difficulties anyway, as other scholars subsequently pointed out in detail (Homer-Dixon 1999; Kahl 2006), the logic of linking security to environment collapses and the case for changing what we mean by security and how we think about achieving it become unavoidable. Deudney (1999a: 214) summarizes his argument by putting the matter very directly in one of the passages that has been most widely quoted in this whole debate:

> Nationalist sentiment and the war system have a long-established logic and staying power that are likely to defy any rhetorically conjured redirection toward benign ends. The movement to

preserve the habitability of the planet for future generations must
directly challenge the power of state centric nationalism and
the chronic militarization of public discourse. Environmental
degradation is not a threat to national security. Rather,
environmentalism is a threat to the conceptual hegemony of
state centered national security discourses and institutions. For
environmentalists to dress their programs in the blood-soaked
garments of the war system betrays their core values and creates
confusion about the real tasks at hand.

Deudney's concern was primarily with matters of national security.
But the possibilities of linking security with humanity more generally, in terms of the UNDP (1994) formulations, or at the largest scale
of global security, suggest that with modifiers other than "national,"
security might still have utility as an argument for action by agencies other than the military. Hence the connection the UNDP (1994)
drew with human insecurity and the global dimensions of many
threats.

In particular, what is crucial to the UNDP formulation is precisely
that they note that new threats are often the unintended consequences
of social, economic, and environmental changes rather than the deliberate threatening actions of foreign states. While this may require
emergency measures and the necessity of invoking security it doesn't
necessarily present an obvious external threat against which to mobi-
lize. On the other hand, however, to update Renner's (1996) earlier
argument about the fragile political order of many impoverished
states, the complex human insecurities there make the possibilities of
political violence more likely. Given the likelihood of natural disasters
to aggravate political tensions, especially when elites fail to deal effectively with the consequences of earthquakes, floods, droughts, and
storms, the potential for "environmental" causes of political disruption
is high (Nel and Righarts 2008). Where political instability arises due
to natural hazards, the old Cold War division between foreign policy
responses to political difficulties and international aid to deal with disasters disappears (Duffield 2007). The discussion of complex humanitarian emergencies and the extended discussion of the "responsibility
to protect" the limits of sovereignty and international obligations to
intervene (International Commission on Intervention and State

Sovereignty 2001) follows on from this, and as we will see in chapter 6, it now needs some further rethinking in light of climate change.

Marc Levy (1995), in another much-cited critique of the environmental security discussion, not only posed questions of the empirical efficacy of the discussion about environmental causes of wars, but put the matter directly in terms of environmental threats to the United States in particular. His argument was blunt in suggesting that environment wasn't a security matter unless it directly endangered the United States or some other major power. The link to narrow, classical realist definitions of security emphasized the importance of the referent object of security and implicitly raised the question of the politics of security. The contrast with the United Nations approach, looking to the insecurity of the most vulnerable people, is clear; but this point about who is threatened by what runs right through the whole environmental security discussion. Busby's (2008) recent discussion of the argument that climate change ought to be a matter of national security for the United States returns to this theme in updated form.

Likewise other fears of biological weapons, accentuated by fears of their use by terrorists in the "war on terror," Malthusian mobs, genetically modified food crops, and numerous technological insecurities are also in circulation in contemporary political discourse. The crucial point that Hartmann, Subramaniam, and Zerner make in concluding their edited volume is that fear is a political matter, even if it isn't explicitly discussed in terms of security:

> While we can be afraid of many things and perhaps should be afraid of yet others, we are taught to be afraid of only certain phenomena. The fears that ultimately consume us are neither random nor the most frightening, We are taught to be afraid of "suspicious" looking people, white powdery substances, and "strange" activities. The color codes of terror are elevated, and yet we are encouraged to move around as "usual" and continue to shop, watch movies, and visit restaurants and bars. On the one hand, we are told to fear alien and exotic plant and animal species because they destroy natural habitats, while on the other hand the dangers of genetically modified food and their impact on natural habitats are underplayed. Contradictions abound. But one thing is clear – threat making is political, and what we are afraid of is the

result of a complex web of ideology; politics; economics; and the social, cultural and natural. The promise of safety and security is illusory. (Hartmann et al. 2005: 247–8)

It's in this larger, pervasive world of fear and insecurity that contemporary discourses of environmental security make their claims of danger requiring action and appropriate policy responses on the part of states and international institutions. Many of these themes of alarm were replayed in the discussion of climate change in the aftermath of Hurricane Katrina and Al Gore's movie *An Inconvenient Truth*. But alarm is not necessarily useful for mobilizing effective policy responses, and the invocation of science to justify alarm frequently is ineffective too (Risbey 2008; Grundmann 2007). As later sections of this book show, the science of all this requires careful evaluation and appropriate contextualization if the general claims to alarm are to be made specific enough to be useful. Simply linking climate to security, without remembering the earlier discussions about the difficulties of environment formulated as a threat, suggests that previous mistakes will simply be replicated.

There are a number of further considerations in understanding how the politics of environmental danger works in contemporary circumstances in the developed world. In particular, these multiple fears and discourses of insecurity are part and parcel of the economic discourses of risk and uncertainty that have infused contemporary policy discussions of everything from bottled drinking water to the fluctuations of the stock market and the 2008 global financial crisis. Not only do the traditional institutions of states get involved in the provision of security but this has now been marketized in private security firms, whether it's household burglar warning systems or virus scanners on our computers, but also more explicitly in the insurance business, where all manner of risks are commoditized and regulated in complex legal and financial arrangements. These literally, to borrow Mick Dillon's (2008) word play on David Campbell's (1998) book title, are "Underwriting Security." Governance and security are morphing into complex market strategies, as neo-liberalism both privatizes and commodifies many facets of our lives in complex technical practices that supposedly provide protection in the face of life's vagaries. Contingencies and the emergence of life itself are securitized and commodified in contemporary modes of governance (Cooper 2006). Or at least they are for those who operate in the commoditized economy; those who have property and the wherewithal to purchase insurance. Security is very much about the economics of risk and the ability to spread the costs of danger through the global economy.

Recent commentators on security have been making very clear that security is about maintaining forms of political order, frequently invoking emergency measures to ensure the perpetuation of modern states and their economic systems and the privileges of the rich and powerful (Neocleous 2008). The invocation of danger to social order is a powerful mobilizing theme in political discourse, but that social order is a larger, more inchoate matter of culture and the identities that apparently need to be protected. Michael C. Williams (2007) suggests security is about symbolic power and the reproduction of modes of political life, not simply about protecting states from external threats. Thus he argues "the culture wars" in the United States in the last few decades were not simply a matter of partisan struggles or purely domestic politics, but spilled over into the conduct of foreign policy and international security, nowhere more obviously than in the Bush administration's adoption of the neo-conservative agenda of military engagement with Iraq and other putative rivals to American predominance in international affairs. But this now becomes all the more complicated because it's precisely this modern culture that has caused the transformation of so much of "nature" that environmental security problems are on the agenda. Insofar as that culture is threatened then security may be invoked to protect humanity from "natural" hazards.

The more or less endless efforts to protect ourselves against nature in some fashion are in part precisely because we have taken the modern assumptions of humanity as apart from nature seriously. R. B. J. Walker (2006) reminds us that this powerful assumption of the separation of humanity from an external nature, which we can then somehow both seek protection from and simultaneously seek to "protect," is a crucial part of what makes us modern. "To imagine that modern man can protect nature or that he can be protected from nature is already to work within a dualism that is at once the great glory of modern accounts of what it means to be a proper, mature, and free human being and the source of great angst and alienation" (Walker 2006: 190). In the aftermath of the Cold War and the events of September 11, 2001, it is now clear that security is no longer a matter that can be reduced to the mantras of national security and the dangers from external antagonists, but Walker's warnings about just how difficult security is to think in these circumstances are a useful corrective to assuming that environment or any other matter can be easily subsumed within such discourses.

One of the themes that repeatedly recurs in the later chapters in this book is precisely that we cannot innocently invoke environment as something we either need protection from or can protect. Neither security nor environment can be taken for granted; one of the advantages of juxtaposing them is precisely that we are then forced to read each against the other and in the process challenge what is conventionally read into both of them. "That environmental problems are also statist/international problems is quite evident. That statist/international problems are environmental problems is quite evident also." (Walker 2006: 200). There has been very considerable discussion in the last couple of decades about genetic engineering, mapping of the human genome, the possibilities of gene splicing to produce new forms of life, and other areas that make it clear that the distinction between humanity and nature, which was first demolished by Charles Darwin and friends discussing evolution in the nineteenth century, really is untenable.

But now, as the rest of this book will explore, it is also clear that the distinction is untenable at the large scale too, that of the biosphere in which we all live. The contradictions implicit in the discussion of nature as in need of our protection come to the fore as discussions of biospheric disruptions shape contemporary ethico-political debate, while simultaneously invoking numerous discourses of "environmental" danger and climate emergencies. But quite how we came to this pass needs much more attention than it frequently gets; this is the topic of the field of environmental history and the subject of the next chapter.

3

Environmental History: Conquest, Colonization, Famines, and El Niño

The clear recognition of the collapse of the distinction between humanity and nature as a plausible mode of political thinking has profound consequences for how both environment and security can now be understood. Or to be more precise, it can have such implications if the logic of the argument is followed through carefully. If environment is no longer taken as a natural, external, given context for humanity then understanding it as an external threat, in the geopolitical logic of Cold War security studies, is no longer a tenable argument. Of course in a crisis it might once again be articulated in a manner that securitizes environment this way, but thinking through the ecological history of humanity, and understanding how our current circumstances have been remade by human action, make it clear that if such arguments are used in future they are not done so innocently.

Neither, to follow Walker's (2006) articulation of the other part of the argument, is it possible to claim that environment can be constrained within the logic of states and the international system. Clearly environmental matters flow across state boundaries in providing fuel, fodder, and food for much of the world's population. International trade has made nearly all states dependent on these flows of commodities; but it means that each state casts an "ecological shadow" over other states where the resources it uses come from (Dauvergne 1997). This pattern of ecological change in one part of the world being part of consumption in other parts ties us all together in links that are part of the transformation of the biosphere that we discuss in terms of environmental security and especially in terms of climate change (Dauvergne 2008).

But for all the hype about globalization and its supposed novelty, these patterns have long roots in the history of humanity's expansion over the globe. How we have come to the present situation of global environmental crisis is in part about our past and how we have colonized the planet in the process of modernization. Environmental history has emerged as a burgeoning field of study in the last few decades. Its topics are diverse, but clearly adding environmental dimensions into the study of humanity's past is a worthy exercise. But interpreting those lessons is not so simple. Linking science, environmental change, archaeology, and anthropology together is a fascinating intellectual exercise. Linking all this to security is particularly difficult, but insofar as lessons from the past might be useful for contemporary thinking and policy formulation, it's a task that needs to be undertaken.

Not least it needs to be tackled because the doom and gloom scenarios that have so frequently structured both alarmist journalism and popular books on themes of environment, as well as more thoughtful academic analyses, frequently don't think through the history of changes carefully. The presupposition that our existing state of things is the benchmark against which future matters ought to be judged ignores the most simple and important lesson of history: things change. Insofar as security is understood as a policy to keep some things the same it may well be a counterproductive strategy. While many things do remain the same, the contexts in which people act are not the same and the recent alterations in the global environment, the subject matter for chapter 4, have changed many things in ways that suggest we have to be very careful about drawing lessons from the past.

More specifically, if we are to draw lessons from history we need to position our analysis carefully in our own historical circumstances to draw attention to which lessons may be appropriate and which may not. We also have the crucial advantage that Jared Diamond (2005) discusses at the end of *Collapse*: the ability to learn from histories that we know about, something many earlier societies facing disaster may not have been able to do. We also now understand just how complicated ecological systems are, and how historical understandings of environment may not now be helpful in understanding what needs to be done, where, when, and by whom. While the prehistory of humanity, and the disruptions caused by climate, volcanoes, and other hazards, are a fascinating tale (Fagan 2004), one which has at times ended in disaster for particular societies (Linden 2007), it's of less direct relevance to the discussion in this book than more recent events. Unless, of course, nuclear war looms again in the short term or we all face imminent climatic catastrophe!

Chapter 1 dealt with the scenarios of doom and briefly with the alarmist possibilities of societal collapse, the ultimate security threat; we will leave those cases aside for the moment and in this chapter mainly focus more explicitly on the historical context within which our contemporary ecological predicament can be understood. The reason is that, as chapter 4 will make clear, the circumstances that face us in the early decades of the third Christian millennium are in many ways, and much more so than in previous societies, those of our own making. Crucially, they are also now on a truly global scale and tied into technological and economic matters that have transformed many facets of human existence. But understanding how we came to make these circumstances is essential to thinking intelligently about global and human security in the future. Not least this is a matter of relevance to contemporary discussions of climate and environmental justice (Vanderheiden 2008). History has much to teach in terms of who caused the problems, and who then has the primary responsibility for devising and implementing solutions in terms of contemporary climate change policy (Roberts and Parks 2007).

Ecological Imperialism

Perhaps the most clear and concise account of the environmental history on the large scale that shapes our contemporary circumstances comes from Alfred Crosby's book from the 1980s simply called *Ecological Imperialism*. His argument was simple and compelling: while conventional history has focused on wars, great men, conquest, and the spread of European power in the last millennium, the rats, rabbits, diseases, horses, and plants that came with the colonizers have transformed the ecology of the planet in many ways that are more fundamentally important to understanding that history, but which frequently don't get much attention precisely because they are not human stories; they don't fit into the conventional way history has been told. But now, as concerns about global environmental change and fears of the security implications of that change are becoming such an important political matter, it is especially important to put that ecological dimension of history into accounts of the past so that the context of the present can be appropriately understood. What Crosby (1986) makes clear is that over the last thousand years the rise of Europe has been a project of ecological transformation quite as much as a matter of armies, navies, kings, wars, and, more recently, technological change.

Part of Crosby's (1986) account is about the destruction of indigenous flora and fauna, and the death of indigenous peoples in the Americas in particular caused by disease. Europeans deliberately brought with them cattle, sheep, dogs, horses, rabbits, and various birds, but they also inadvertently brought disease microbes. Diseases such as smallpox arose from the ecologies of animal domestication across the world as agriculture expanded and food sources became a matter of cultivation, breeding, and production rather than harvesting (Diamond 1997). These diseases devastated some of the populations that they were introduced to; most noticeably in the Americas where the population had no immunity to smallpox, tuberculosis, and other hazardous micro-fauna. On the other hand, when Europeans encountered some tropical areas with diseases to which they were not immune, settlement was more or less impossible until the nineteenth-century medical innovations made it possible for many immigrants to survive. Imperialism is a matter of diseases and the geographical ranges of their vectors, such as mosquitoes, quite as much as it is about military conquest or economic exploitation.

However, the other side of the coin is the construction of new ecologies as a result of the introduction of species from afar. Ships not only brought wheat and horses, rats and rabbits, with them to the new worlds, but also returned with tobacco and potatoes to Europe. Sugar, coffee, tea, and numerous other commodities changed lives the other side of the world; these commodities were key to the expansion of imperial power. European merchants grew rich on this trade and in the process simultaneously changed the habits of consumption in the metropoles while transforming the ecological conditions in what became colonies abroad. In the process, plantation agriculture too transformed habitats in many places; a pattern that is being currently re-invented in attempts to plant trees to "sink" carbon emissions from metropolitan countries (Lohmann 2006). Agricultural products are now flown around the world every day taking advantage of climatic niches and global transportation systems, but the pattern was set in motion as part of the expansion of European power.

The agricultural transformation of habitats is not only a matter of plants and crops but also one of the domestication of animals and birds as part of an artificial ecological ensemble which has facilitated the spread of humanity (Diamond 1997). Cows, goats, sheep, dogs, and chickens are only the most obvious members of the domesticated Euro-Asian species mix that allowed humanity to expand. Norse adventurers colonized Greenland and lived there in very marginal circumstances for hundreds of years largely because they brought livestock with them to turn grass into edible products. Their survival there in harsh circumstances suggests immense tenacity in the face of great difficulty. But it also suggests, at least to Jared Diamond (2005), that they failed to adopt the Inuit ways of life that might have allowed biological survival when a cooler climate in the little ice age period made European farming impossible; culture defined them as European and Christian and as such probably limited their adaptability.

Diseases are an unavoidable part of human history, but one that has had very substantial impacts on geopolitics in the last few centuries. European diseases were key to the destruction of indigenous populations in the Americas; they frequently spread through populations prior to the actual arrival of the soldiers. The military destruction of societies already devastated and disoriented by disease was relatively easy for the conquistadors. But European soldiers also frequently were vulnerable to diseases in the tropical regions, and at least in the case of yellow fever this had no small role to play in the geopolitics of Atlantic America (McNeill 2007). Many casualties in the imperial campaigns of the British army were from disease; both Asia and Africa held off foreign invaders until the nineteenth centuries by the inability of most Europeans to survive in these climates. But in the case of the initial conquest of North America by Europeans it was the invaders who had the bacteriological advantage.

As colonization extended and in some cases exterminated species by hunting, as in the case of the beaver in large parts of North

America, ecological niches opened up to new possibilities. One simple example will have to suffice as an illustration of a much larger process of transformation. William Cronon (1983) points out that new ecological opportunities came in the case of abandoned beaver ponds. After the widespread hunting killed off the beavers, their dams across New England that had previously enclosed small lakes subsequently collapsed. Frequently they exposed accumulated silt on the valley bottoms, which were then quickly converted into very fertile agricultural land. This wasn't an instantaneous or planned innovation; but ecological opportunity presented itself later as an unintended consequence of hunting the beaver. Subsequently many of these farms in New England were abandoned in the twentieth century and were either turned into towns and highways or reverted to forests as trees once again spread over the landscape. The larger lesson to be drawn from this example is the simple one that environmental change is just that, and while in the short run this might be understood as a matter of degradation and a species loss in terms of beaver eradication in the region, in the long run a new, artificial ecology was produced, and eventually forests recolonized the abandoned fields.

Timber has long been used by humanity the world over as a fuel source for heating, cooking, and smelting as well as for construction. Forests have been drastically reduced if they have not disappeared altogether in many places as urban civilization expanded (Chew 2001). This is not only because of the clearance of land directly for agricultural use but was, until well into the nineteenth century, also a matter of timber supplies for shipbuilding. Timber supplies and their control played a substantial part in European rivalries and the British navy's attempts to control the Baltic sea among other places (Michael Williams 2007). Subsequently timber has been used for numerous construction purposes, furniture, and more recently on a huge scale as the source of pulp for paper. But it is important to note that deforestation is a major terrestrial land-cover change that has been directly caused by human activities. Naval strategy is no longer concerned with ensuring the supply of large trees for masts, spars, and all the other timber needed for ship construction in the age of sail. Strategic resources change as construction technologies and modes of propulsion change.

In more temperate climates the British in particular succeeded in establishing settler colonies where immigrants brought with them their agricultural technologies and turned prairies into what Crosby (1986) calls "neo-Europes." Canada, the United States, New Zealand, South Africa, and, in part, Argentina effectively became extensions of the European agricultural system. Elsewhere plantation agriculture provided sugar, tea, coffee, cotton, and numerous other commodities to the growing European economies. But in the process Crosby emphasizes the importance of what he calls the portmanteau biota, the "scaled down" combination of animals and plants that Europeans took with them first to the Canary Islands, where they took over from the existing biota, and subsequently elsewhere. The combination didn't work in some places, especially where disease prevented humans and animals from spreading. In some places, like the great plains of North America, direct extermination of the local animals was necessary to destroy the livelihoods of the remaining indigenous human populations and clear the way for cattle and horses. But the overall effect was to drastically change substantial parts of the planetary terrestrial biota. Environmental change is tied directly into the expansion of particular human modes of living; hence Crosby's (1986) apt title *Ecological Imperialism*.

All this became much more important as the late nineteenth-century transportation technology, first the sail-powered clipper ships and subsequently the steam-powered freighters, integrated the agricultural production of food and materials with the factories and markets of Europe. As trade in grain in particular became routine, the global ecology became much more immediately interlinked with human affairs. Ironically it was at this stage in the latter parts of the nineteenth century that environmental determinist arguments became popular. Culture was linked to nature and attributes of particular cultures were explained in terms of their climatological circumstances rather than in terms of a larger series of interconnections of political economy (Deudney 1998, 1999b). But what was not clearly understood in these discussions was the variability of non-European climates, or the fact that temporal rhythms other than the seasons that dominated European agriculture might be important to ecologies elsewhere (Flannery 1995).

Late Victorian Holocausts

As the global market for grains spread around the world as part of the expansion of industrial capitalism, and as European empires grabbed large parts of the world, they turned them into colonies to supply the metropoles with numerous commodities. The violent disruption of Africa as part of the slave trade and the elimination of millions of people in what later became the Congo are just part of the reorganization of the planet driven by the expansion of trade and conquest (Hochschild 1998). The emergence of the Third World, what we now more or less term the global South, is thus the precursor to much of the vulnerability of the people now inhabiting what Mike Davis calls the *Planet of Slums* (2006). Recognizing that vulnerability is tied into the spread of globalization is key to thinking about policies that might tackle the causes of human insecurity.

Mike Davis (2001) tells the dramatic story of the huge famines that struck many parts of the world in the late 1870s and subsequently in 1888–91 and again in 1896–1902, and in the process shows the part played by the dramatic transformation of the global economy in the period. "We are not dealing, in other words, with 'lands of famine' becalmed in stagnant backwaters of world history, but with the fate of tropical humanity at the precise moment (1870–1914) when its labor and products were being dynamically conscripted into a London-centered world economy. Millions died, not outside the 'modern world system,' but in the very process of being forcibly incorporated into its economic and political structures" (Davis 2001: 9).

Indeed the economic policies of liberal capitalism, when applied in India and elsewhere, only made matters worse. In the aftermath of droughts and famines, imperial powers in the nineteenth century expanded their reach into the lands whose societies were disrupted by the catastrophes. In British-ruled India, rather than railroads and the new communication technologies of the time facilitating the distribution of grain to alleviate starvation, they facilitated the transport of grain to central depots out of reach of many of the starving and greatly aided speculation in grain prices. Food security was now about having the cash to buy grain, not about traditional patterns of mutual aid, and the careful hoarding of supplies in case of future shortages.

"Suddenly the price of wheat in Liverpool and the rainfall in Madras were variables in the same vast equation of human survival" (Davis 2001: 12). Government policy, orthodox in its following of doctrines of non-interference in the marketplace, did little to ensure supplies to starving people. The relief camps, where weakened people were forced to do hard labor for meager wages, turned into extermination camps as the absence of hygiene and lack of nutrition doomed inhabitants to death. Nothing, it appeared, had been learned by the imperial administrators from the failures to deal with famine in Ireland three decades earlier that had killed over a million people and forced another million to migrate abroad.

The disruptions in the world grain supply coincided with a period in Britain when wheat production had declined, and the stage was set for a rapid expansion of grain production abroad where new lands were opened up for production. "With the British demand for food imports soaring, massive amounts of London-generated capital flowed into the railroads that opened up the American Great Plains, the Canadian Prairie, the Argentine pampas, and India's upper Gangetic plain. Maxim and Gatling guns efficiently eradicated the last indigenous resistance to the incorporation of these great steppes into the world economy" (Davis 2001: 119–20). The expansion of the neo-Europes, in Crosby's (1986) phrase, was completed in this period, the Wild West was tamed, and the cavalry completed their mission. Elsewhere these events coincided with the scramble for Africa (Hochschild 1998) and the expansion of European and American imperial interests, as the steamship and railroad incorporated much of the world into an economy where the metropoles were becoming enriched at the expense of the dispossession and reorganization of the conquered lands to supply commodities to the world system.

For the purposes of the discussion here, the additional point of Mike Davis' (2001) account is that he links these factors up with the then emerging science of climate. As meteorological statistics became available in the latter part of the nineteenth century, correlations across different parts of the world could be made and the erratic patterns of what are now understood to be ENSO events, where El Niño is linked to Southern Oscillation, charted. But in the latter years of the nineteenth century this perturbation in global climate then intersected with the emergence of a commercial economy in grain, and many millions died in India, Brazil, China, and elsewhere. By focusing on the unreliability of the monsoon, a fickle and stingy nature could be blamed for the famines where millions died.

In the twenty-first century, especially if it turns out that global warming affects the oceans in ways that enhance ENSO events, then the disruptions of climate variability will be part of the future food system. Now, in addition to being vulnerable as a result of the capriciousness of markets, the poor and marginal people, who are the victims of famine because of poverty and a lack of social entitlements, may turn out to be doubly vulnerable insofar as the system from which they are economically excluded is precisely the system that renders them subject to now more extreme weather events. These events, while driven at the largest scale of the global atmosphere and oceanic systems, have very local consequences, not least as a result of orographic effects where mountains intercept moving clouds bearing moisture, but also of precisely where people actually live.

Now the displacement of rural populations and the wholesale migration into the growing cities of the South frequently place people in harm's way. The poor frequently have little choice as to where they can live, being forced to take whatever piece of ground they can find to erect some form of shelter. More affluent people with the options of buying or renting in more established market systems usually end up on flatter ground, less likely to be subject to landslides and flooding. (Of course there are many exceptions to this tendency, as residents of California in particular seem prone to building in fire ways or on cliff tops subject to erosion.) But blaming "nature," as in suggesting that floods are a "natural" disaster and that people are victims of forces that they are powerless to combat, overlooks the social and economic circumstances that put people in harm's way in the first place. Environmental determinism remains a potent explanatory trope, not least because it looks so obvious and removes the necessity for complex explanations.

The contrast Davis (2001) draws between on the one hand the disasters of the late nineteenth century in China when millions starved, and again in the late 1950s when Maoist policies utterly failed to deal with the famine of that period, and on the other hand earlier widespread crop failures of the 1740s, when the spring monsoons failed two years in a row, is especially instructive. While mass starvation happened in the later events, it didn't happen in 1743–4, when a comprehensive relief effort was organized with rations given to the two million peasants in the affected region. When local stores were exhausted, large quantities of rice and millet were moved from the south northwards to Zhili and northern Shandong to ensure that the social contract with the peasantry was maintained. The contrast with the contemporaneous situation in Europe in the 1740s, where many starved as a result of climate disruptions there, leads Mike Davis (2001: 281) to acidly summarize matters thus: "In Europe's Age of Reason, in other words, the 'starving masses' were French, Irish and Calabrian, not Chinese." This experience in China in the 1740s built on a track record of careful attention by the bureaucracy to supplies and preventing price speculation to ensure food security for the population. The contrast with subsequent reliance on markets in later centuries, or, as in the case of the 1950s famine, official denial that the event was even occurring, is noteworthy. The Qing period took infrastructure provision seriously and actively worked on agricultural diversification and flood control. One hundred and thirty years later the system had neither the financial or grain reserves to assist in a disaster, nor the political mechanisms in place to coordinate relief.

The expansion of global trade networks and the penetration of imperial rule into many rural areas in the latter part of the nineteenth century dramatically altered subsistence systems, and relatively speaking, tropical commodity prices fell as market integration reduced the bargaining power of peasantry vis-à-vis merchants who were increasingly integrated into global financial systems. The expansion of large commercial farms, the enclosure of common spaces into private commercial production arrangements, and the erosion of traditional survival systems by market forces all led to increased vulnerabilities, the gradual migration of impoverished and dispossessed people to urban centers, and the growth of disparities between the developed metropoles of the global economy and the increasingly impoverished peripheries, a pattern that has been replicated repeatedly as modernization transforms rural areas and propels urbanization (Gadgil and

Guha 1995). Many marginal producers in the late nineteenth century turned to cotton as a cash crop, attempting to supplement incomes or, in the face of food crop failures, provide the necessary cash to buy food. But once again they were simultaneously at the mercy of the weather on one hand, and of the prices merchants in the cotton trade were prepared to offer on the other. The price in turn depended on what happened in the Southern United States that year, the major cotton-growing region in the global economy, and vulnerabilities to climate were compounded by vulnerabilities to price mechanisms over which rural producers had no control.

The appearance of what subsequently became known as the Third World was accelerated by these "late Victorian holocausts," and in many places the prior successes in ameliorating the vulnerabilities of rural populations were forgotten. Doctrines of environmental determinism were formulated in this period attributing numerous cultural traits to the climatic conditions peoples lived in, and in the process both disparaging non-European cultures and feeding larger discourses of Orientalism, with their viewpoints that rendered the European experience the norm from which others were judged (Said 1979). The Third World discourse then subsequently naturalized the peasantry as poor, vulnerable, and in need of development, all the while ignoring the political ecology of vulnerability that modernity had wrought.

Third World peoples became "the people without history," the conquest and disruptions of imperialism ignored in the stories of modernity triumphant (Wolf 1982). Environmental determinism suggested that they died because of stingy nature, not as a matter of political economy. That stingy and dangerous nature also indirectly provided a geopolitical vocabulary of wild, dangerous, and threatening places beyond the remit of civilization's taming and pacifying hand (Lipschutz 1997). These themes persist to this day in the way Africa in particular is rendered as a dangerous place, one frequently in need of intervention, both an alluring and a dangerous other (Dunn 2003). It is the source of key materials for the global economy, but a dangerous, threatening, foreign place, the antithesis of civilization increasingly understood as modern, urban, and technological. Above all these are places that would later be understood as being in need of development.

Something New Under the Sun

The simultaneous transformation of metropolitan societies and their overseas colonies is key to the processes in the nineteenth century that shape our contemporary situation. All this becomes clearer in J. R. McNeill's (2000) careful synthetic analysis of our new historical condition; in his words, borrowed from the biblical phrase in Ecclesiastes, there now is *Something New Under the Sun*. That's us. McNeill starts with the nineteenth century insofar as its dominant coal-powered industrial mode of production, what he terms "Coketown" following Charles Dickens' designation in the novel *Hard Times*, set the context for the emergence of twentieth-century, petroleum-powered "Motown," based on the automobile production complex centered in Detroit. Here what Lewis Mumford (1934) termed "carboniferous capitalism" has been extended from the industrial heartland of the industrial revolution, first in Britain and subsequently to Europe, America, and then Japan, into a petroleum-driven (literally!) urban civilization connecting all parts of the planet (Paterson 2007). Dams, oil wells, chlorofluorocarbons, floods, the green revolution, deforestation, urbanization, and many other aspects of environmental change are interwoven in the narrative; this is the point of environmental history; it shows how all these things interconnect. McNeill's (2000) overall argument is that humanity is changing the global biosphere as a result of its economic activity. Hence there really is something new under the sun; the environmental context for human life is being remade by human activity.

While the industrial revolution set in motion the steam-powered commercial networks of railroads and ships that linked the global economy much more intimately and quickly together, it also set in motion a military revolution where steam power and steel produced a whole new mode of naval warfare. Coal stations now became a key part of military logistics. But they in turn were to be quickly replaced by petroleum supplies for navies, and not incidentally the long history of British concern with Middle East oil supplies has its genesis in this technological innovation. The industrialized slaughter of the two twentieth-century world wars followed on from this, expanding the range of ecological disruption as resources were mobilized in many places to feed the war machines; but ironically too giving the oceans' fish, and whales in particular, a temporary reprieve in the early 1940s. Commerce raiders, and later submarines, made long-distance fishing much more hazardous than in previous years. Military systems continue to use large amounts of resources, alienate tracts of land for training grounds, and generate all sorts of pollution and hazardous substances, a legacy that continues now not least in such things as depleted uranium munitions left on recent battlefields (Singer and Keating 1999).

Most of the oil for the Allied effort in the world wars could be supplied by the United States, still then the world's largest producer of petroleum in the early 1940s, but not for much longer. The rise of a global trade in petroleum, which has come to be such an important matter subsequently, has its origins in this conflict, when for the first time gasoline and diesel fuel were crucial military supplies. The huge advances in vehicle design and in aviation made during the war set in motion the postwar expansion of the global economy. The car had started transforming transportation in North America in previous decades, reducing both the environmental impact of urban horses and the huge cropland devoted to supplying oats, but the spread of the car after the Second World War, and the huge infrastructure provision of highways, urban roads, car parks, and gas stations, not to mention the massive use of energy and materials to manufacture them, had a major impact on all aspects of the global economy. While cars were to be followed later by electronics, televisions, music systems, computers, and endless kitchen gadgets, the transformation of economics into a petroleum-powered world set in motion the rapid increases in carbon dioxide levels in the atmosphere, with all the disruptions of climate change that are now coming to fruition. In McNeill's (2000: 310) words "The automobile is a strong candidate for the title of most socially and environmentally consequential technology of the twentieth century. Cars in 1896 were such a curiosity that they performed in circuses along with dancing bears; by 1995 the world had half a billion cars." Since then private automobiles have spread rapidly in China, where they were only made legal in 1984, and in India too, where they are once again sold as a status symbol quite as much as a matter of practical use.

Simultaneously with the expansion of highways, dams, coal- and oil-powered electrical grids expanded; dams have blocked the natural flows of most of the large rivers on the planet to at least some degree. The controversy over the Three Gorges dam project in China is simply the latest major controversy over the costs and benefits of these dramatic changes to the hydrosphere. Drilling technology and diesel-powered pumps have allowed agriculture and cities to extract water from underground aquifers in many places, facilitating food production in arid climes, but doing so in a way that exhausts the reservoirs sooner or later. Likewise the huge use of water for industrial purposes, and the expansion of urban sewage systems, have modified water use but also allowed the treatment of many of the worst cases of water pollution. Water is no longer a natural matter; it is a commodity that is purified, managed, controlled, metered, and sold in all sorts of complicated technical practices.

Another innovation derived from the Second World War that has had far-reaching transformative effects is the standardized shipping container. Combined with the ships, trucks, and trains to move it, this system has facilitated the rapid expansion of global trade and the building of manufacturing plants in many parts of the world, allowing the commodity chains of European empires to be transformed into a truly globalized production and trade system. Most recently the rise of China as a global manufacturing center has focused attention on the trans-Pacific trade of all manner of consumer items, a trade that involves so many freighters and containers moving so much material across the ocean that it too can easily be understood as a new physical process in the biosphere. Air transport is also part of this global economy, allowing luxury goods to be flown round the world: flowers for Valentine's day in London from Kenya or Israel, or, as Australian Friends of the Earth (Spratt and Sutton 2008) ruefully note, fresh California spring cherries in the food markets in Melbourne.

While these economic processes have expanded globally so too has the human population. Just as the industrial revolution in Britain and then Europe involved a massive influx of people into the new industrial towns to work in the factories, while subsistence farms and common grazing lands were enclosed in the larger commercial agricultural enterprises of the time, so too are rural people moving into the large cities of the global South, although only a small fraction of the migrants find jobs in the new export processing zone factories. This process of migration is in part caused by the expansion of commercial agriculture that feeds the cities, displacing traditional people and practices and replacing them with industrial methods, monocultures, irrigation schemes, pesticides, and new seed varieties of the green revolution and now genetically modified varieties used as feedstocks for numerous new food products that are traded on the world market. But it is a system based on fossil fuels, both to operate the equipment and move grain, animals, and produce to market, and as a feedstock for the crucial fertilizers that perpetuate the production of crops well beyond what the natural fertility of the soils could provide.

The ecological imperialism of earlier centuries has thus morphed into a much larger pattern of global transformation. Ecological change is part of the processes of the colonization of all corners of the world by the contemporary system of world economy, one that still is mostly powered by fossil fuels. Given this widespread propensity to turn rocks into air, which is what we do every time we drive a car, even if we don't think about it in quite these terms, it seems eminently appropriate to extend the term "carboniferous capitalism" to summarize the ecological consequences of contemporary economic activity (Dalby 2002). What is also clear from this analysis is that conflict is perhaps inevitable as dramatic transformations of the natural systems and people's modes of living, property arrangements, and customary practices are dramatically disrupted by the expansion of modernity into rural areas. Whose security is protected in these processes isn't necessarily clear, and assuming conflict is a matter of scarcity, rather than dislocation, may dramatically misconstrue the causes and appropriate policy options for anything approximating a program of sustainable development (Peluso and Watts 2001).

World Systems and Environmental Change

Crosby's (1986) discussion of the expansion of European power and the construction of what he calls the neo-Europes fits into the current attempts to link environmental history explicitly with questions of global political economy, and into the discussions of the world-system approach to history with its emphasis on the integrated and connected human condition, where human society is understood as differentiated across the world but linked together by trade and politics (Hornborg et al. 2007). Putting the pieces together is a major scholarly task, and historians are hard at work making the connections between environmental factors and humanity. In retrospect it is possible to think through how such things as the expansion of sugar-cane production in Latin America is related through disease to geopolitics (McNeill 2007), or how the history of deforestation in Europe and North America in the last few hundred years is related to struggles for naval power and access to crucial materials needed for shipbuilding (Williams 2007). Connections between global commodity prices and access to suitable land to grow the crops or extract minerals are key to the historical patterns of political economy, which are also of course environmental transformations. Hence the rise in the use of the term "political ecology" in the last few decades as geographers and other scholars try to tease out the struggles to gain wealth and power and the ecological changes tied up in these processes (Peet and Watts 2004).

The colonial resource extraction patterns of the nineteenth century accelerated in the twentieth and have continued to expand in the first few years of the twenty-first. Richard Tucker's (2007) overview of the consequences of American imports of ecological resources is bluntly titled *Insatiable Appetite*. The pattern of imports from the tropical world into the United States is the key focus in this analysis. While some products could be grown in temperate climates, others require tropical climates to grow; hence they have to be imported. Sugar from sugar cane is imported because demand is so high that tropical sugar cane is drawn on in addition to temperate climate sugar beet. Bananas are popular and have to be imported, and numerous plantations in the tropical world to feed this demand have had ecological repercussions (Lipschutz 2004). Likewise coffee, which is now ubiquitous in American culture, is also a tropical crop. Natural rubber too; but rubber was crucial as a source of military material, like other strategic minerals, at least until synthetic rubber was made from petroleum in the Second World War to deal with the shortage of imports, not least because of the wartime Japanese occupation of Malaysia and other tropical sources. Beef imports have likewise had ecological impacts as expanding grasslands and croplands to feed the cows have caused deforestation in many places. Finally in Tucker's (2007) list are tropical hardwoods, used in many ways in the United States. All of these trading relationships have made ecological changes far from where the commodities are consumed. This ties environmental degradation into economics at a distance, and as such makes it clear that ecological matters cannot be discussed solely within the administrative conveniences of national boundaries.

But this is not a matter solely of the United States; other economies are drawing tropical produce into their consumption systems, and in the process effectively exporting the environmental consequences of their economies. Particularly salient in all this in the 1980s was the deforestation of Asia by Japanese business interests. Peter Dauvergne's (1997) analysis of this emphasizes the failure of external businesses to invest in the local economies from which they extracted timber. Without any serious attempts to make the production of timber sustainable, but rather a pattern of buying logs, no questions asked, from local traders who may or may not have been behaving in either a legal or a sustainable manner, the timber trade cast long ecological shadows over the countries of South East Asia, initially the Philippines but later also Thailand, Malaysia, and Indonesia. When coupled with international demands for pulp for paper production, the overall effect of these patterns is to degrade forests in many places. Given the important ecological functions of forests, such patterns of extraction are especially worrying when viewed at the largest scale of the global forest economy (Marchak 1995). They are so too because urbanization is related to a very long history of deforestation (Chew 2001).

Likewise the European states that once were the centers of empires stretching across the globe have not given up importing resources and commodities from tropical climes. The alarm in Britain in early February 2008 when violence convulsed Kenya, concerning whether the workers in the fields and greenhouses of Kenya would be able to harvest the flowers that are an essential commercial part of St Valentine's day, emphasizes the global spread of such commodity chains. But coffee and numerous vegetables also come from Kenya to Europe. Not all of this is necessarily harmful in an ecological sense; an additional argument in circulation in discussions of flower imports suggests that flowers flown from Kenya may use less energy in total than those grown in fossil-fuel-heated greenhouses in Europe. As researchers at the Wuppertal Climate Institute in Germany have made clear, one key to lowering total human ecological impact is to import products that are produced sustainably and that help development in the poorest parts of the world while stopping the trade in minerals and other substances that degrade Southern ecologies (Sachs and Santarius 2007).

Not only are resources exported to the North from tropical climes potentially damaging to the environments where they are produced, but in some cases it seems these patterns of exports are directly related to violence in the South. Where there are few economic alternatives for populations living in poverty, and huge revenues to be gained by those who can control the rent streams from the export of resources, the incentives to fight for control over the resources directly, or maneuver politically to gain benefits from the states that have large resource revenues, are high (Michael Ross 2004). Thus the violence related to struggles to control diamonds in Sierra Leone, oil and timber in Angola, and numerous other minerals and petroleum supplies is related fairly directly to the global political economy (Renner 2002; Le Billon 2005). The violence of the new wars of the twenty-first century is in part about controlling these flows of supplies to the global economy (Kaldor 2007).

The global resource conflicts that are frequently invoked are mostly about oil these days, and seem likely to be about oil for the foreseeable future. They are obviously about the situation in the Persian Gulf, and in South West Asia in general. They are about old patterns of geopolitical rivalry, about the persistent attempt on the part of the American elites to use military force to control the trade in oil in the region (Klare 2004; Bacevich 2005). The efforts to find new sources of oil, and the persistent rivalries over controlling supplies and the huge profits to be had from oil when the price is high, have focused attention once again on Africa as a source of raw materials for the global economy, and suggest one more "scramble for Africa" is currently underway (Carmody and Owusu 2007).

But none of that suggests that a global war for resources is being fought as such, at least not yet, although discussions of access to the Arctic and its petroleum deposits, especially in light of the rapidly receding polar sea ice, suggest that claims to territory and resources will be part of future political struggles (Klaus Dodds 2008). In the Middle East the ability to control the flow of petroleum to Asia is undoubtedly a key component in strategic thinking in Washington, where China is understood to be an emerging geopolitical competitor. The ability to even realistically threaten to cut off fuel supplies in a crisis could give Washington a very important leverage in the future (Harvey 2003).

But oil isn't about scarcity at the margins; it isn't about violence caused by shortages, but about control over an abundant resource that is the key to so much in the global economy. The global economy spreads such conflicts across national boundaries so impacts of consumption in one place are frequently displaced into other states and regions (Adam Simpson 2007). Petroleum may be about control over the global trade and about who controls access to the particular sources of supply, but this is not a resource that the marginalized peasantry of the Third World are directly fighting over; it's a matter of superpower competition for a resource that is becoming more difficult to extract while ironically its accelerated use is compounding difficulties of greenhouse gas emission (Klare 2008).

Environmental Security in a Globalized World?

On the smaller scale it's frequently the rural poor in many places that find themselves in the way when large energy projects are set in motion to fuel that global economy. Insofar as they resist they too can be considered part of the relationship between environment and conflict, but once again it's not about scarcity or environmental resources; rather it's about their being in the wrong place as far as development is concerned (Gedicks 2001; Evans et al. 2002). Where violence occurs in struggles over the impacts of "development projects" it is also worth noting that the conflicts in many cases may be about arguments over compensation for the disruptions of traditional livelihoods, at least as much as direct opposition to the "development" (Walton and Barnett

2008), an important point that might be most useful for at least some peacebuilding and human security policy initiatives.

This point might become especially important in the coming years if bio-fuels are promoted as the solution to both oil dependence and greenhouse gas emissions, and this in turn further accelerates the spread of large-scale industrial agriculture that displaces subsistence farmers and small-scale producers. The spike in food prices in 2007 and 2008 round the globe suggests that this combination may already be beginning to constrain food availability for the poor, and discussions of food riots are once again in the news. But how such conflicts play out, and how they might turn violent, are usually context dependent. This is related to the institutional structures that facilitate or prevent adaptation; here too climate change may aggravate difficulties caused by poor distribution of food in some places (Barnett and Adger 2007).

But such considerations are a long-standing matter of development, of rural change as commercial systems challenge and replace traditional modes of economy. Working out how this happens is a matter for anthropologists, geographers, and other social scientists who are sensitive to context, fieldwork, and the small scale (Bohle 2007). But this does not provide for easy-to-generalize data of the sort that quantitative analyses by economists interested in cross-national comparisons might consider appropriate scholarly method (Korf 2005, 2006). Neither does a focus on small-scale field studies necessarily resolve matters; as some researchers have discovered, even small rural communities that might reasonably be assumed to be largely dependent on local resources are frequently more tied into the larger operation of the commercial economy than expected (Haag and Hajdu 2005).

All of which suggests the sheer complexity of matters related to resources and the great difficulty scholars have in formulating appropriate notions of scale in all this (O'Lear and Diehl 2007; Dalby 2007a). How to contextualize is made especially difficult when it's clear that the global economy ties so many places together in commodity chains that span the globe (Dauvergne 2008). Fish caught in one ocean are landed in a port on the coast of another, frozen, and shipped back across the seas to be processed into all manner of frozen products elsewhere. Likewise grain and minerals and all manner of materials are on the move, so that assumptions about local shortages and abundance are increasingly a matter of trade as much as they are one of proximate ecologies. Boycotts and "fair trade" certifications, policy instruments related to "blood" diamonds, and international campaigns on such matters as working conditions and child labor make it clear that many resources that are in conflict in one way or another are in some senses unavoidably "global" (Le Billon 2007).

Borders and nation states also become difficult in the matter of carbon offsets and the attempts by many policy-makers to "sink" carbon emissions from fossil-fuel use in the global "North" by using forestry plantations in the "South." This might fairly directly link global consumption to very local conflict where land uses are dis-rupted and people relocated to make way for the plantations. This pattern of resource exploitation in the peripheries of the global economy isn't a new trend either, even if it is now justified by various "green" rationalizations (Lohmann 2006). Once again the causes of such violence are about the expansion of the larger global political economy rather than obviously indigenous causes of conflict (Roberts and Parks 2007); getting the geographies of this clear is important if metropolitan policies are to be considered in terms of their likely peripheral impact.

All this matters because, as we become an urban species, it is crucial to put these transformations at the heart of discussion if the causes of vulnerabilities are to be understood in the appropriate historical context of the remaking of the world by carboniferous capitalism. It's in the context of that remade world that contemporary vulnerabilities have to be understood and the appropriate policy lessons drawn for how security can now be understood. As the contemporary scientific evaluations of the state of the planet are making clear, transforma-tions on a global scale are underway that render security of many kinds subject to environmental change.

4

Global Change and Earth-System Science

Trying to tease out the connections between history, environment, and security is all the more complicated when the global dimensions of the climate system are worked into the picture, but as chapter 3 showed, the fascinating story of El Niño and the interconnection of climate with human vulnerability are essential to understanding the links between environmental change and security in various ways. Now as the debate about climate change continues, its relevance for contemporary times and for the immediate future is unavoidable. If parts of humanity in the past have been vulnerable to the climate system, what of the contemporary world that is now increasingly being shaped by human actions? If climate change induces perturbations in the earth's biosphere in ways that are not predictable, but which could be disastrous for substantial parts of the human population, what does this mean both for humanity's future and for how we think about both environment and security?

This isn't a matter of climate change alone. As chapter 3 also showed, humanity is changing many facets of the earth, not just the atmosphere. What is also becoming clear is that these various changes are connected together into what is now frequently simply called the earth system. Discussing climate change has made it clear that ocean, land, and air are interconnected more closely than was traditionally understood. The sheer scale of human activities has made it clear that what matters now is the whole biosphere as an integrated system that includes us, and that we are changing as we follow economic policies of "development." Increases in atmospheric temperature are related to ocean temperature rise, which in turn may provide more energy for hurricanes and other storms. Land-use changes, clearing forests in particular to make way for farming, changes the climate as albedo and evapo-transpiration rates change. These changes also involve the movement of nutrients and water. Hence both the difficulty and importance of trying to understand these things in specific places and simultaneously understanding how all the specific places link up in larger trends. These interconnections are the context of environmental change within which we now have to rethink security.

Precisely because of the complexity of these factors it is clear that any straightforward argument about environmental degradation causing insecurity or conflict is oversimplified. Likewise the global interconnections make it clear that changes in one part of the biosphere may have impacts elsewhere. Scale matters here; so too does the complexity of adaptive systems. At the largest scale, that of the biosphere, it is becoming clear that humanity is a new force changing ecological arrangements. In doing so we are disrupting numerous ecological phenomena while simultaneously producing new artificial contexts for human life in the rapidly growing cities, and in the global economy that links these cities to each other and to the rural hinterlands that provide the food, fuel, and commodities for those cities. Increasingly those hinterlands also provide the beaches, parks, and other tourist locations that urban dwellers seek so they can recover from the stresses of their urban existence. The fuel urban dwellers use in these adventures, and in particular the rapid rise in aviation, is also part of the environmental changes that are caused by carboniferous capitalism.

The sheer volume of scientific material now being published on matters of global environmental change, or on topics that have at least indirect implications for how we think about environmental change, is huge and cannot be adequately encompassed in this chapter or even in the whole book. To cope with the volume of material that might be relevant this chapter looks at the highlights of a number of recent scientific overview reports, most of which in one way or another build on the findings of the historical analysis discussed in chapter 3. This chapter also briefly links this science with some directly related current discussions of the possibilities of these environmental changes to cause insecurity and in particular some forms of violence. Here we pick up the brief discussion of the 2003 Pentagon scenario study on climate change and potential future wars in chapter 1, and link that theme into more recent scientific thinking.

Global Environment Outlook

In its most recent *Global Environmental Outlook* (*GEO*) report, published in 2007 (*GEO4*), the United Nations Environment Program has explicitly focused, as the report's subtitle indicates, on environment "for" development. Rather than argue that environmental damage hinders development, the suggestion is that it's a matter needed for development. But if healthy environments are necessary for development, the clear indication in the *GEO4* report is that in many places they are not available. While climate change is perhaps the overarching concern for the United Nations, in the words of Ban Ki-Moon, the United Nations secretary-general, in the foreword to *GEO4*: "Many other clouds are on the horizon, including water shortages, degraded land and the loss of biodiversity. This assault on the global environment risks undermining the many advances human society has made in recent decades. It is undercutting our fight against poverty" (2007: xvi). Published 20 years after the Brundtland commission summarized the arguments for sustainable development (WCED 1987), *GEO4* looks back at changes since 1987 and then looks forward in a discussion of environmental trends in terms of the atmosphere, land, water, and biodiversity. In each case, while matters have changed and some useful innovations have been adopted, there are worrying trends suggesting that many things have not improved. Which pointedly raises concerns with larger troubles ahead.

While carbon dioxide emissions are a key focus because of their role as greenhouse gas, other matters such as urban air pollution have important impacts on health and economy too; estimates of up to two million premature deaths as a result of air pollution are noted. While agreements in the 1980s and 1990s to phase out the production of chlorofluorocarbons, and action by some states prior to the full importance of ozone depletion being recognized, all helped, it is still the case that even with full compliance with international agreements, the ozone layer over the Antarctic will not fully recover until 2060 at the earliest. Other innovations are noted, in particular the increased efficiency with which carbon fuels are used, but these improvements are counteracted by the rapid increase in use of these fuels, especially in aviation. In May 2008 it was announced, on the basis of data from the Muana Loa observatory in Hawai'i where these things have been tracked since 1958, that the carbon dioxide levels in the atmosphere had reached 387 parts per million, and that the accumulation of carbon dioxide was accelerating, not slowing.

Land use for crops has expanded since the Brundtland commission published its report, but while the rate at which newly cultivated land is added to agriculture has slowed, the intensity of use of existing land has increased notably, at least some of which is not sustainable. Persistent pollutants contaminate many places, and while better emission controls are in place in many developed states, where industry has been established in newly developing states pollution is frequently a problem. Forest ecosystems are threatened by increasing human demands, and land degradation, nutrient depletion, and the disruption of biological cycles are persistent concerns. Water depletion due to agricultural use compromises land quality in many places while desertification in degraded dry lands is also an issue. Pressure on land resources is likely to increase, but the authors suggest that sensible policies can adapt farming methods to deal with many of the difficulties.

Water is essential to life and the availability of clean fresh water for agriculture, sanitation, and industrial purposes is constrained in many parts of the world. Current projections suggest that shortages and water stress are likely to increase in coming decades. Quality will also decline unless measures are taken to reduce contamination and protect water sources. Fish, which provide food for many, depend on aquatic resources too. Numerous fish habitats have been disrupted and fishing stocks depleted by overfishing. The complexity of the management problems where environmental services often rely on the same sources of water as development projects is noted in the *GEO4* report. Ocean pollution, warming, and acidification are also issues, not least because oceans provide a large sink for atmospheric carbon dioxide, while industrial, urban, and agricultural runoff pollutes coastal seas. Coral reefs and coastal areas are also directly vulnerable to tourism developments, which disrupt ecosystems, not least in removing mangroves and coastal wetlands to open up beach resorts.

Air, land, and water all come together in discussing matters of biodiversity. Understood in terms of the basis of ecosystems and their services to humanity, the biodiversity concept incorporates both the range of species and their quantity; it is quite simply "the variety of life on earth. It includes diversity at the genetic level, such as that between individuals in a population or between plant varieties, the diversity of species, and the diversity of ecosystems and habitats" (United Nations Environment Program 2007: 160). As habitats are destroyed, numerous species have been forced into extinction. This process is driven by land-use change and the appropriation of plants and animals for food and other uses, and is happening at an increasing rate. Once species are gone their genetic possibilities are no longer available either to subsistence farmers for food or medicine, or for commercial production. Development options are precluded by the decline in biodiversity. Where market systems only value commercial crops and ignore ecosystem services provided by other species and undisturbed ecosystems, the tendency to eliminate biodiversity continues to the long-term detriment of humanity, which cannot replace the lost ecological possibilities when ecosystems are destroyed. While ecosystems can recover from numerous disruptions, once species are removed permanently ecosystems simply do not have that specific genetic material with which to rebuild.

Millennium Ecosystem Assessment

One of the most comprehensive recent studies of the biosphere and its component ecosystems is the Millennium Ecosystem Assessment (MA 2005a, 2005b), a project that emerged from the United Nations Millennium deliberations. Its comprehensive overview ranged around the world synthesizing the peer-reviewed scholarly literature on ecosystem health. In recognition of the crucial importance of the human dimensions of contemporary ecosystems, "The conceptual framework for the MA posits that people are integral parts of ecosystems and that a dynamic interaction exists between them and other parts of ecosystems, with the changing human condition driving, both directly and indirectly, changes in ecosystems and thereby causing changes in human well-being" (MA 2005a: 9). Clearly this is not the whole story; natural changes unrelated to human activities also continue, and so too human innovations that may not necessarily have obvious ecological consequences. But the MA's (2005b) five volumes, which outline in detail, region by region, changes in ecological circumstances, make it clear that very substantial changes to numerous parameters are underway.

The overall assessment suggests both that we are clearly damaging numerous ecosystems and that we have already driven many species to extinction. In the process we have caused a sizable and largely irreversible reduction of earth's biological diversity. It also notes that only now are we beginning to understand these processes in detail.

> Everyone in the world depends completely on Earth's ecosystems and the services they provide, such as food, water, disease management, climate regulation, spiritual fulfillment, and aesthetic enjoyment. Over the past 50 years, humans have changed these ecosystems more rapidly and extensively than in any comparable period of time in human history, largely to meet rapidly growing demands for food, fresh water, timber, fiber, and fuel. This transformation of the planet has contributed to substantial net gains in human wellbeing and economic development. But not all regions and groups of people have benefited from this process – in fact, many have been harmed. Moreover, the full costs associated with these gains are only now becoming apparent. (MA 2005a: 16)

More specifically, the assessment suggests that about 60 percent of the earth's ecosystems are not being used sustainably and that the current changes hold out the prospect of non-linear changes in the future. These may bring surprises that disrupt human systems too. Indeed the summary findings emphasize that the costs of human changes are disproportionally borne by the poor and disadvantaged. In Africa in particular the health of ecosystems is clearly related to the fate of people relying on subsistence agricultural systems for sustenance (MA 2005a: 17). Frequently these people are made more vulnerable by the disruptions caused by the commercial agriculture that feeds people elsewhere, but these consequences are frequently not noted. Achieving the United Nations Millennium Development Goals (MDGs) is especially difficult in these marginal circumstances. "More generally, any progress achieved in addressing the MDGs of poverty and hunger eradication, improved health and environmental sustainability is unlikely to be sustained if most of the ecosystem services on which humanity relies continue to be degraded. In contrast, the sound management of ecosystem services provides cost-effective opportunities for addressing multiple development goals in a synergistic manner" (MA 2005a: 17).

The MA emphasizes the speed of the changes in the last half century. More land was converted after the Second World War ended in 1945 than in the previous two centuries combined. Half of the artificial fertilizer used on earth since its introduction in 1913 was used in the two decades after 1985. As much nitrogen is now being "fixed" artificially as is occurring in "natural" processes. The total amount of phosphorus moving through the biosphere has tripled since 1960. Although data is limited, where it is available it suggests that more than a third of the mangroves on earth have been destroyed since 1945 too. The rapid increases in agriculture are key to this, and with that has come a large increase in the withdrawal of water from rivers and lakes, and the construction of numerous dams and irrigation works that have changed terrestrial hydrology dramatically.

The sheer scale and speed of all these things happening simultaneously are key to the reduction of biodiversity as numerous species lose habitat because humanity's appropriations expand. Demand for food, water, fiber, timber, and fuel drives these ecosystem disruptions. While these agricultural activities have improved the lot of many people, they have frequently come at the expense of the poor and marginal, and also at the cost of future generations who may not have the ecosystem services available when they need them. Sixty percent of fish ecosystems are being unsustainably harvested, and ground-water supplies in particular are being used well beyond their replenishment rates in many places. While precise estimates of these matters are difficult to tabulate, the overall trend is very clear in the data.

In addition to these concerns the MA assessment emphasizes that market mechanisms frequently underestimate ecosystem costs of resources use. Disruptions that don't register on the bottom line are usually ignored even though they may be of higher value than what enters the market. Decisions are made on market criteria with other matters not considered. Lack of ecosystem services may lead to everything from eventual loss of revenue to floods, fires, and the spread of pathogens, with all their associated human costs. Above all the loss of ecosystems is a loss of a capital asset for future generations; economic growth now may well be at the price of future generations if species, water systems, and soil fertility are damaged or destroyed. The benefits accrue to the users of the food, fiber, and water, and to the corporations that trade these, but the local population frequently bears the costs.

Thus development of this sort is not sustainable because what future generations may need will not be available thanks to the actions of present economic systems. When ecosystem integrity is under-mined in some places it directly hampers the achievement of the MDGs. How to make environment and development compatible in at least some senses thus emerges yet again as a pressing question. The contradiction at the heart of the sustainable development discussions in the 1980s is therefore once more on the agenda, but in the context of this systematic evaluation of the world's ecosystems, one that is an ever more pressing priority for billions of the poorest of humanity; precisely those who most need the benefits that development prom-ises; those who are in other words the most insecure. Looming over all this is the discussion of climate change and the growing recognition that the world is undoubtedly warming (Hansen et al. 2006).

The Intergovernmental Panel on Climate Change

The implications of climate change became a high-profile issue in 2007, when numerous reports on the issue made their way into the public arena, and the United Nations discussed the related security issues in April that year. Most high-profile of all was the discussion around the "Fourth Assessment Report" (FAR) of the IPCC. the final version of which appeared late in 2007. In part because of concerns about conflict as a result of climate change, this scientific effort earned the IPCC scientists a share of the Nobel peace prize in 2007. While it had become apparent to climate scientists in the 1980s that green-house gases were apparently causing warming (Schneider 1989), there remained considerable doubt about both the evidence and the computer projections that were being used to examine likely effects of a warmer planet. Work on collecting evidence, and on building models that can accurately predict climate changes, has continued apace for the last two decades.

In the process the IPCC effectively became the international clearing house for the science, and it drew on numerous experts in many fields to synthesize knowledge and issue summaries of the state of the science. Given the political opposition to arguments about climate change (Jacques et al. 2008), the IPCC review process has been very thorough and the assessments are conservative in the sense that they only report matters on which there is very clear evidence and wide agreement among scientists. As such the reports err on the side of caution and are anything but alarmist about the science of climate change. The scenarios where predictions about human consequences of climate change are discussed are inevitably tentative, but the physical models do have some clear indications of what is coming, and in particular they suggest that the current warming in polar regions will continue.

Earlier reports, in 1990, 1995, and 2001, had synthesized research findings and updated assessments as more results became available, but by the time the FAR appeared in 2007, the evidence that human actions were causing greenhouse gas emissions and hence climate change had become overwhelming. The synthesis report of the IPCC fourth assessment (IPCC 2007: 30) which summarizes its results was quite clear: "Warming of the climate system is unequivocal, as is now evident from observations of increases in global average air and ocean temperatures, widespread melting of snow and ice and rising global average sea level." More than this, "Eleven of the last twelve years (1995–2006) rank among the twelve warmest years in the instrumental record of global surface temperature (since 1850)" (IPCC 2007: 30). This has had different consequences in different parts of the globe, but the report continues:

> The temperature increase is widespread over the globe and
> is greater at higher northern latitudes . . . . Average Arctic
> temperatures have increased at almost twice the global average
> rate in the past 100 years. Land regions have warmed faster than
> the oceans . . . . Observations since 1961 show that the average

temperature of the global ocean has increased to depths of at least 3000m and that the ocean has been taking up over 80% of the heat being added to the climate system. (IPCC 2007: 30)

The list of changes continues with a comment on shrinking Arctic sea-ice area, a trend that came to widespread notice in September 2007 when for the first time in recorded history the North West Passage, in northern Canadian waters between the Pacific and Atlantic oceans, was ice free. Other indicators of change in the polar regions all point in the same direction of dramatic warming: the seasonally frozen ground area has decreased; so has the area of snow cover; permafrost is shrinking and glaciers are melting too. Rainfall, with all the implications that has for floods, droughts, and agriculture in particular, has also been changing: "Trends from 1900 to 2005 have been observed in precipitation amount in many large regions. Over this period, precipitation increased significantly in eastern parts of North and South America, northern Europe and northern and central Asia whereas precipitation declined in the Sahel, the Mediterranean, southern Africa and parts of southern Asia" (IPCC 2007: 30). Clearly if such trends continue the viability of agriculture in places which dry out may be in jeopardy.

The IPCC efforts to generalize these trends are limited by a paucity of data in many places; developing countries just don't have sophisticated data-collection systems on many facets of environmental change. Hence the caution with which the assessment reports have summarized information and the caution with which they suggest the environmental changes that have resulted from climate changes. But in the FAR they are willing to state with high confidence that climate change has caused glacial lakes to grow, spring runoff to come earlier, and numerous other changes to hydrology related to snow and ice melting. Likewise they are confident that biological changes, such as earlier spring leaf growth, can be attributed to climate changes too. Water temperature changes have affected fish migrations and the range of numerous aquatic species. In short there are demonstrable changes in the biosphere related directly to the warming planet. They affect water supplies and vegetation growth as well as sea levels, and show every indication of accelerating in coming decades.

Teasing out the human implications of these and similar earlier IPCC findings has not proven easy and much work remains to be done on understanding the interconnections of climate and human activity. Much of the work has focused on scenarios for the future and projections on a series of assumptions about the future rate of warming. Plugging these assumptions into climate models, seeing where environmental change happens in these imaginary futures, and then drawing reasonable inferences as to how societies will react is an inexact science at best, but it at least suggests the kind of implications and plausible planning that might usefully be undertaken, because it is now clear that changes are real and already happening. More importantly they are accelerating, and this crucial point is the cause of much alarm in the scientific community.

All this is now getting more attention in the media and among policy-makers because the FAR seems to have finally convinced most of the skeptics that climate change is real and has been happening for some time now. Through the 1990s and into the 2000s an orchestrated campaign of what became climate-change denial influenced both media discussion (Boykoff and Boykoff 2004) and the practical politics of dealing with the Kyoto protocol and other international agreements in Washington (Mooney 2007). Pointing to uncertainties, and doubts about the veracity of data and the assumptions in computer models, this muddied the policy agenda with arguments that effectively delayed action on greenhouse gas emissions by the Clinton and subsequently the George W. Bush administrations. But by 2007, however reluctantly, most governments seemed to have conceded the argument and now accept that climate change is real and needs to be addressed by policy-makers. How to go about this is, however, far from agreed upon, and the huge international climate-change negotiations underway to attempt to build an international agreement to deal with climate change after the Kyoto protocol expires in 2012 do not suggest that progress will be rapid. Nonetheless, insofar as the IPCC matters, getting a broad consensus that climate change is happening is an essential first step to silencing doubters and allowing policy to be considered.

A very substantial part of the difficulty in teasing out the existing impacts and the implications for future changes is the simple but crucial point that climate change is only part of the picture. As both the MA and the *GEO* documents make clear, humanity is changing other dimensions of the biosphere simultaneously. Land-use changes, ocean-wide fishing, agriculture, and urbanization are all going on concurrently and humanity is adapting to these changes too. As far as thinking about the relationship between security policy and environmental change is concerned, the complexity of these multiple changes makes any attempt to reduce matters to some generalized indexes much less useful than detailed empirical studies of particular places (Barnett et al. 2008). This is so because societies are different and the particular circumstances they face are just that: particular, despite the obvious fact that all places are subject to global changes. The point is that they play out differently in different contexts, and how institutions, including security institutions, react depends to a large extent on how local dangers are specified by political leaders. But while many political leaders are concerned about security they are, especially in the poorer parts of the world, much more concerned about development.

Human Development

Both the authors of the UN Environment Program (2007) *GEO4* report and those of the UNDP *Human Development Report 2007–2008* (UNDP 2007) draw on the IPCC figures in thinking ahead about the implications of climate change. The *Human Development Report* addresses the question of climate change directly, suggesting in the subtitle of their report the need for *Human Solidarity in a Divided World*. It's a concern for development workers precisely because recent achievements, and in particular practical development work in the immediate future to meet the United Nations MDGs, may be disrupted by climate change. Thinking about such things as clean fuels and renewable energy is part of the agenda, but resources may be diverted to deal with flooding and droughts. Developing weather-resistant strains of crops may need attention too; thinking now about the likely effects of climate change so these plans are put in place to adapt to it is part of the challenge, but slowing down change is essential: "While we pursue adaptation we must start to reduce emissions and take other steps at mitigation so that the irreversible changes already underway are not further amplified over the next few decades. If mitigation does not start in earnest right now, the cost of adaptation twenty or thirty years from now will become prohibitive for the poorest countries" (UNDP 2007: vi).

The emphasis on costs of adaptation is at least partly misplaced, the United Nations authors argue, because large-scale investment in new technologies will have all sorts of payoffs in economic terms in addition to avoiding the worst impacts of climate change. But recognizing the need to focus on innovation and remaking economies so they do not emit greenhouse gases in huge quantities long into the future are essential if development is to continue and the future for much of humanity is not to be compromised.

> The early warning signs are already visible. Today, we are witnessing at first hand what could be the onset of major human development reversal in our lifetime. Across developing countries, millions of the world's poorest people are already being forced to cope with the impacts of climate change. These impacts do not register as apocalyptic events in the full glare of world media attention. They go unnoticed in financial markets and in the measurement of world gross domestic product (GDP). But increased exposure to drought, to more intense storms, to floods and environmental stress is holding back the efforts of the world's poor to build a better life for themselves and their children. (UNDP 2007: 1)

This relates directly to the distributional issues and who specifically is rendered insecure by climate change. The poor who have not caused the emissions of greenhouse gases are the most vulnerable. The politics of insecurity here is very directly related to environmental change.

> In rich countries, coping with climate change to date has largely been a matter of adjusting thermostats, dealing with longer, hotter summers, and observing seasonal shifts. Cities like London and Los Angeles may face flooding risks as sea levels rise, but their inhabitants are protected by elaborate flood defence systems. By contrast, when global warming changes weather patterns in

the Horn of Africa, it means that crops fail and people go hungry, or that women and young girls spend more hours collecting water. And, whatever the future risks facing cities in the rich world, today the real climate change vulnerabilities linked to storms and floods are to be found in rural communities in the great river deltas of the Ganges, the Mekong and the Nile, and in sprawling urban slums across the developing world. (UNDP 2007: 3)

But how specifically do these vulnerabilities play out, and what are the precise mechanisms that link environmental changes to disruptions of development? The UNDP report suggests five principal connections. First and perhaps most direct is the link between climate, agriculture, and food security. Rainfall reductions and drought in vulnerable regions – and Africa is probably the most vulnerable area in this regard – directly reduce food availability for producers; famine is not unknown in Africa but the potential for more widespread malnutrition is especially worrying. Second, water stress and insecurity result from changing rainfall patterns, and in Asia in particular retreating glaciers in the Himalayas may reduce water availability in coming decades. Third is the question of rising sea levels and direct exposure to climate-induced disasters, floods, hurricanes, landslides, and vulnerabilities in the huge urban slums of the megacities of the South. Biodiversity losses and ecosystem disruptions are the fourth concern; coral reefs in particular are showing bleaching effects from changing ocean temperatures, and some species simply can't adapt or move in the face of the scale and pace of ecological change. Fifth are the direct implications for all this in terms of human health and the possibilities of diseases spreading in areas that have limited public health capabilities; malaria and dengue fever already seem to be expanding their range. Put together, these changes directly impact on people's security in many ways. A development agenda that deals with efforts to reduce emissions of greenhouse gases to mitigate climate change while simultaneously building adaptation into development strategies is called for. This will have to be a global effort that makes innovations that are appropriate in specific places; carbon-fuel reductions in North America, flood-protection devices in the Netherlands, low-water-use irrigation systems in many places.

The Future: *GEO4* Scenarios

But what might the future look like? What are the implications of this science? How do we think about the future intelligently so that policy decisions now head off the worst threats? These are familiar questions to military and security thinkers whose job is to plan for future contingencies and build institutions, train troops, and make weapons, transport, and supply systems available to deal with war if it comes (Dalby 1996). Much of this involves scenario construction, imagining a series of circumstances in which the worst happens, and then working backwards to think through what needs to be done to prepare to respond to imminent and not so imminent threats. In the world of strategic planning the frequent assumption is that if these preparations are made they may well deter potential foes from attacking. Deterrence is part of the calculations of military and security planners. But here at least the parallel with traditional security planning might appear to break down. After all, the threat that we need to face is our own doing, not something that can be pinned on an external military or a state with evil intent.

On the other hand, strategic thinking also has to deal with the security dilemma wherein "our" preparations for defense are seen by others as threatening, which in turn requires "them" to prepare, which then in turn makes "us" even more worried about "their" intentions; and so on in a cycle that induces both military preparations and not a small degree of paranoia. In the case of climate change "our" actions in the developed affluent world, where security is studied, and books on security written and read in universities, are directly threatening to people in poor states who are more vulnerable, and directly threatening to future generations whose options will be drastically curtailed if nothing is done to alter existing trends in greenhouse gas production. But unlike traditional security studies, those whom we threaten – the poor in the global South, or our as yet unborn grandchildren and great-grandchildren – are not planning to defend themselves; nor do they have the ability to threaten affluent Northern states in any plausible manner. They don't have armies that can invade; they don't have navies or air forces to transport those non-existent armies either. In the long run, however, with sea-level rise, disasters increasing, and major disruptions to agriculture and the global economy, the affluent societies that have set these trends in motion will be directly affected too.

To try to grapple with the likely impacts of climate change, the IPCC has used scenarios in which various assumptions about the use of fossil fuels and the increase in greenhouse gases are made. Then these are worked into the increasingly sophisticated computer climate models to see what changes might happen. While the models have been criticized for all sorts of reasons, increasingly accurate predictions are becoming possible so at least broad generalizations about how environments will change in the future can be made. The *GEO4* (United Nations Environment Program 2007) report draws on some of the IPCC scenarios in trying to tease out likely scenarios for the future. More specifically, it does so to investigate policy options and their likely implications. Four scenarios are presented with different policy emphases: "markets first"; "policy first"; "security first"; "sustainability first." Given the theme of the report, which is trying to suggest that environment is a crucial necessity for development, it is not surprising that the scenario that gives the only chance of turning things around in the coming century is the sustainability one. However, it might not be so obvious that giving security priority turns out to be disastrous. The key to this is, of course, what kind of security for whom and in what kind of future?

The "markets first" scenario focuses on maximizing economic growth and on extending the power of markets to enhance the total size of the economy. Markets and trade get priority and much of the remaining world commons gets taken over by corporations. Ecosystem services are ignored in favor of the commodities that can be extracted and sold. Trade trumps international environmental agreements and no effective follow-up to Kyoto is implemented when it expires in 2012. Growth of industrial agriculture continues to cause land degradation. Water supplies for the poor suffer as priority goes to commercial expansion of supplies, and despite technical innovations the amount of untreated sewage continues to grow in poor areas. Biodiversity suffers as climate change and infrastructure cut into habitats.

"Policy first" priorities retain the focus on growth but introduce top-down central government initiatives to clean up the worst of environmental pollution. The inability of markets to deal with eco-system services becomes clear and a focus on long-term health investments and the gradual eradication of perverse subsidies deals with some problems; the widespread designation of protected areas solves some biodiversity losses. Oil and gas continue to dominate a growing energy economy and water stress is a problem in many places, which requires large-scale investments to decrease demand and enhance supply. Climate change and the expansion of agriculture, not least to feed bio-fuel industries, leads to loss of habitat and biodiversity; fishing down the food chain in the oceans does the same there too.

"Security first" focuses on keeping the existing distribution of power and wealth intact, paying attention to the environment only insofar as it is understood as a source of resources for the global economy. It's a narrow view of security, which enhances controls on migration but facilitates the expansion of trade. Private security companies flourish as freedoms are restricted, and official and foreign direct investment get low priorities. Protecting habitat gets little attention and coal technology has a resurgence that increases atmospheric pollutants and greenhouse gas emissions. Climate change puts further strain on food production and water availability, and conflicts in Africa in particular are aggravated by these shortages. Disease spreads too, and valuable coastal ecosystems are destroyed by the aggressive expansion of mariculture.

Sustainability, in stark contrast, focuses on investments in local initiatives to improve human wellbeing. It's not a rejection of private-sector initiatives but involves a focus on equity, transparency, and legitimacy of all actors, and above all the assumption that all levels of government actually follow through on commitments to address both social and environmental matters. The Millennium Declaration and MDGs are key, linking justice and environmental responsibility, fair trade and socially responsible investment. But the scenario also assumes that people take initiatives and don't wait for governments to act. Investments in water infrastructure are important in this scenario, while biodiversity protection is integrated into sustainable harvesting in many ecosystems. Solar and wind energy gradually catch up with oil as an energy source and the use of oil begins to decline. This means that climate change remains a problem, but less so than in other scenarios, because changing energy use slows and eventually levels off carbon dioxide concentration in the atmosphere. Integrated water management tackles quality and quantity issues simultaneously.

These scenarios point to some of the consequences of policy choices being taken now, but how these will play out is of course not clear, not least because politicians learn and circumstances change. The extent of climate change is dependent on greenhouse gas emissions. Water stress in regions depends both on infrastructure to meet demand and on how climate changes may influence the supply. But these matters too have a regional dimension; climate change isn't a neat linear progression, neither is humanity evenly spread across the planet. How changes interact with specific human circumstances is key to thinking about the future and how development and security will play out in specific places.

Whatever happens in terms of the four scenarios, in Africa population increases will remain an important part of the picture in coming decades. Sustainable energy strategies will be needed regardless of what scenario plays out, but integrating environmental thinking into development is needed to ensure that land degradation doesn't hamper wellbeing. In Asia the "security first" scenario suggests that the breakdown of governance structures may aggravate many environmental difficulties and compromise water supplies and fishing. In contrast, new cooperative arrangements are key to a sustainable future, although investments in technology will be important in this region. Migration into Europe is a particular uncertainty in all the scenarios given the aging population there; the "security first" scenario could lead to a reduction in environmental controls and a diminishing of effectiveness of the European Union. Latin America and the Caribbean suffer from serious problems of inequality and indebtedness, which need to be dealt with but might be aggravated in markets and "security first" scenarios.

Urbanization is a key driver in all the scenarios here. North America, with its high use of carbon fuels, might change rapidly if consciousness of the need for sustainability caused rapid innovation in industrial production that reduced carbon-fuels use and began to tackle the diffuse consequences of sprawl and the increasing strain on water resources. West Asia suffers especially in the "markets first" scenario, but "security first" might lead to persistent conflicts that make dealing with environmental matters much more difficult. Water stress is likely to remain an issue across the region. In the polar regions climate change is a persistent and dominant issue and will remain so through the coming decades, but whether indigenous people are empowered to tackle the huge changes they face, or the polar regions become a zone of geopolitical confrontation, depends on which scenario plays out.

Earth-System Science and the Anthropocene

With so many interconnections and the growing realization that the scale of human activities is having widespread repercussions, and in ways that are not necessarily predictable, questions of how to synthesize the findings in numerous human and social sciences inevitably emerge.

> The interactions between environmental change and human societies have a long and complex history, spanning many millennia. They vary greatly through time and from place to place. Despite these spatial and temporal differences, in recent years a global perspective has begun to emerge that forms the framework for a growing body of research within the environmental sciences. Crucial to the emergence of this perspective has been the dawning awareness of two fundamental aspects of the nature of the planet. The first is that the Earth itself is a single system, within which the biosphere is an active essential component. In terms of a sporting analogy, life is a player, not a spectator. Second, human activities are now so pervasive and profound in their consequences that they affect the Earth at a global scale in complex, interactive and accelerating ways; humans now have the capacity to alter the Earth System in ways that threaten the very processes and components, both biotic and abiotic, upon which humans depend. (International Geosphere Biosphere Programme (IGBP) 2001: 4)

Attempts to piece together a comprehensive knowledge of the biosphere have been made in recent years frequently under the rubric of "earth-system science" (Steffen et al. 2004; Schellnhuber et al. 2005).

These key findings are crucial to understanding the context for think-ing seriously about human security in the future. They effectively piece together the various concerns in the United Nations documents discussed in this chapter and suggest most clearly that thinking about environmental change has to be done in a way that takes the increas-ingly artificial circumstances of humanity seriously as its starting point.

First, a generation after James Lovelock (1979) suggested as much in his formulation of the Gaia hypothesis, earth-system thinking notes the crucial, and relatively new, realization that life partly regulates the biosphere; it's an active part of the multiple processes that shape our world. Life is not, as it has frequently been understood to be until recently, a mere addition to a planet of oceans, atmosphere, and rocks. It has actively changed the biosphere, nowhere more clearly than in producing the oxygen that is key to the life of most, but not all, life forms. Thus environment cannot now be understood as something outside of life, or as the given context for humanity. The key separa-tion that most of modern life has assumed, of humanity separate in importance senses from nature on the big scale, no longer makes any scientific sense.

Second, the important point is that the sheer scale of human activities is already now adding a new dimension to these earth processes. It is more than just climate change: "Human activities are significantly influencing the functioning of the Earth System in many areas; anthropogenic changes are clearly identifiable beyond natural variability and are equal to some of the great forces of nature in their extent and impact" (Steffen et al. 2004: 4). Where the first finding suggests that life itself changes its context – that what we have called environment is substantially a product of life itself – now this second finding makes it clear that humanity has become a major factor in shaping the context of life.

The third key finding notes that the various changes to the earth system intersect and may do so in ways that have "cascading" effects. In short, changes in one part may have effects that influence others, with, in turn, knock-on effects elsewhere. Thus analysis has to try to understand these interconnections while also seeing the potential for "cascades" as whole sequences of change are set in motion. The sheer complexity of ecological systems makes this difficult to predict, and analytical science that narrows a focus to examining a small part of life in detail has to be complemented by synthetic work that puts the particular parts back into the larger context. In this it is loosely parallel with the discussion of security complexes in the literature on global security, where particular local phenomena have to be understood as parts of larger patterns of power (Buzan and Waever 2003).

Change doesn't necessarily happen in simple patterns, nor does change of one factor necessarily cause a similar change in others. Systems frequently have thresholds, which when crossed cause abrupt changes. This fourth finding emphasizes the importance of learning where the thresholds in ecological systems are so that dramatic changes don't come as surprises, and in many cases so that policies can be put in place to prevent crossing the threshold in the first place. We learned about one crucial threshold by accident in the 1980s when it was discovered that previously unknown chemical processes were seriously damaging and endangering the stratospheric ozone layer, which blocks incoming ultraviolet "B" radiation from the sun. While most of us know its results as a matter of sunburn, too much UV-B kills numerous forms of life. The damage to this crucial ecological layer came as an entirely unintended consequence of humanity's production of chlorofluorocarbons. These chemicals had been thought to be benign, but they turned out to be both potent greenhouse gases and, when they broke down in the stratosphere over the poles in winter, key to removing the ozone from the upper atmosphere.

Finally, and for the purposes of the analysis in this book probably the most important finding, the changes that we have already caused in the biosphere have pushed some of the key ecological processes of the planet out of the range for which we have detailed knowledge from the past. Over the last six hundred thousand years detailed records of temperature and the composition of atmospheric gases show fluctuation within a fairly narrow range. Carbon dioxide and methane in particular are fairly closely correlated with temperature through this period, which includes a series of ice ages. Reduced greenhouse gases coincide with ice ages, slightly higher concentrations with the warmer so-called interglacial periods, the most recent one of which has provided the relatively stable climatic conditions that allowed the emergence of human civilization. Nowhere in that period of recorded geological history is there any record of methane and carbon dioxide levels at current levels. There is no parallel situation that we might draw lessons from; in the scientific terms of the IGBP (2001) authors we are in a "no-analogue state."

This ecological science makes it clear that we live in new circumstances that are increasingly a matter of our own making. The assumption of an external environment that somehow influences human activities is not a useful starting point for thinking about security or environmental change, and certainly not for how these things fit together. Taking this science seriously as the basis for policy discussion is now essential; environment as a taken-for-granted backdrop for human affairs is no longer sensible in discussions of security of any kind. To encapsulate this new state of affairs and to simultaneously emphasize the importance of the human factor in shaping the biosphere, Paul Crutzen (2002), who won a Nobel prize for chemistry for his work on the ozone layer, and other scientists have suggested that we designate current times in terms of a new geological era. They suggest naming it the Anthropocene, a term that now finds widespread endorsement from earth scientists (Zalasiewicz et al. 2008). This emphasizes the new human "forcing mechanisms" that are driving change in the biosphere.

Obviously, given the discussion of environmental history in chapter 3, there is in some senses an arbitrary quality to precisely when it might be said that the Anthropocene started. Forest burning, the spread of agriculture, rice cultivation, hunting large animals to extinction, the presence of lead deposits in Greenland ice due to smelting in the period of the Roman empire, and many other things all suggest a major human presence shaping the biosphere well before the industrial revolution (Ruddiman 2003; Claussen et al. 2005). But the key point that is usually emphasized is the emergence of wide-scale fossil-fuel use in the industrial revolution period, first in coal-powered industrial power, and subsequently in steam-powered trains and shipping. These innovations of carboniferous capitalism began what has become a worldwide transformation of rocks into air, a geological reversal of hundreds of millions of years of carbon sequestration from the atmosphere by living processes. This reversal adds the new geological dimension to our predicament, hence justifying the designation Anthropocene based on fossil-fueled industrial processes. Subsequently the widespread use of petroleum and natural gas has, in the period since the Second World War, set in motion a "great acceleration" in the changes to planetary processes, effectively launching a second, more dramatic phase of the Anthropocene (Steffen et al. 2007).

The key point about the Anthropocene is that we are remaking the biosphere. Whether we have being doing so since the end of the last ice age and the Holocene is in fact more appropriately named the Anthropocene, as Ruddiman's (2005) hypothesis might suggest, matters little for the argument in this book. The assumption that has structured modernity – that of humanity either apart from, or in charge of, nature – is no longer a valid assumption. Presupposing the environment as something external to our urban societies simply reproduces a long-standing and now outdated formulation that separates humanity from its surroundings. Quite clearly we are part of a biosphere that we are actively changing, and we now need to think about security while recognizing this simple but crucial fact.

The postmodern condition is one where nature is no longer out there either threatening or being controlled directly or indirectly. We are part of nature, it's part of us, and both are changing at an accelerating rate. Slowing down that rate of change, mitigating the forces of climate change, would undoubtedly be a very helpful policy, but adaptation is also clearly essential; we have little choice but to adapt to the climatological changes our colonization of the planet has already set in motion.

Anthropocene Security 1

When discussions of disasters and the urban fate of humanity are linked to the discussions of earth-system science, the big question is one of whether further bigger disasters will be our fate in future. Many of these themes come together in the overview of climate change and security published by the German Advisory Council on Global Change (2008) in their report on *Climate Change as a Security Risk*. This comprehensive attempt to think through the possibilities for the future emphasizes the geographical diversity in which climate change may impact humans in different places, and suggests that there may be numerous modes in which conflict will be aggravated by change. Most obviously, weak and fragile states are poorly equipped to deal with the impacts of climate change, only most obviously the impact of storms, as the population of Myanmar discovered in May 2008 as Cyclone Nargis devastated the south of the country. But if geopolitical rivalries emerge as China and India's power increases in coming years, then deadlock on dealing with either poverty or climate change is a dangerous possibility. The security framework needed in the immediate future is one that works on a peaceful, cooperative, geopolitical transition and simultaneously on institutions that can deal with climate change.

Even if urgent attention is given to climate change, in the short run temperature changes are inevitable because of the increase in greenhouse gases and warming of the oceans that have already happened. If central Asia warms, Africa dries, and the polar regions continue warming, as many of the climate-change scenarios suggest will happen, societies will inevitably adapt. But if, as seems likely given the sheer complexity of the system, global climate responds in a non-linear fashion because it has crossed a tipping point, then much more dramatic consequences may happen in the coming decades. The German Advisory Council (2008) notes that the most discussed non-linear response is the North Atlantic current slowing or stopping, the scenario used in the 2003 Pentagon study (Schwartz and Randall 2003) discussed in chapter 1. Four other likely major system responses are also discussed by the Advisory Council: instability of the West Antarctic ice sheet; instability of the Greenland ice sheet; collapse of the Amazonian forest; and the possibility of the crucial monsoon pattern in Asia being transformed.

The North Atlantic current weakening, which the IPCC 2007 assessment suggests has a very high probability of happening if climate change abatement isn't taken seriously, might not, however, lead to the large, temporary cooling in Europe that Schwartz and Randall (2003) discussed, because the scale of greenhouse gas emissions would be such as to compensate for the loss of warm water off Europe's shores, although if the current broke down permanently cooling might nonetheless occur. Losses to the very productive marine ecosystems in the region would be severe and this would further restrict food supplies. The larger consequences of such a massive shift in oceanic circulation are hard to predict.

Massive shifts in atmospheric circulation systems too might well occur, and if they do perhaps the most dramatic disruptions may occur as the monsoon system is transformed. Much of Southern Asia depends on these wind patterns to bring the rains each year, which supply rice crops in particular with their key moisture. Nearly half of the world's population is at least partly dependent on this food system, so if the monsoon patterns change then much of humanity's food supply is potentially vulnerable. The monsoon is also connected in part to patterns of ocean circulation, as the El Niño phenomenon made painfully clear in the past, and especially in the Victorian holocausts, but better science is needed to make precise predictions in the long term on this phenomenon.

Ice-sheet stability near both poles is also an issue of importance, as it appears that positive feedback mechanisms might cause melting far faster than earlier estimates had assumed. Melt water seeping down from a warming surface may lubricate the flows of ice sheets toward the sea; as large sheets, and Greenland's in particular, shrink, the surface lowers and then encounters warmer air at lower altitudes, so speeding melting. As the melt water from land-based ice flows into the ocean it causes sea levels to rise. Greenland's ice cap alone has enough water in it to raise ocean levels 7 meters. The Arctic has clearly warmed in recent years; 2007 was the first year in which the North West Passage was open to navigation; it's unlikely to be the last. Ocean-level changes aren't likely to happen as quickly as other phenomena, but if storm surges related to hurricanes and other storms happen on top of higher sea levels then the potential for coastal inundations increases too.

Finally, the German Advisory Committee (2008) notes that nonlinear changes also happen in terrestrial ecological systems, and perhaps the most significant of all might turn out to be the Amazon rainforest. While the scenarios are hotly debated, the crucial mechanism is one in which drought affects trees as a result of larger drying of tropical air masses. Given that much of the rain that falls in the

Amazon is derived from local transpiration from trees, dryer air masses alone would probably take some time to have an effect. But coupled with forest clearing for agricultural land and for tree products, which dries out the land and facilitates the spread of grasses and grass fires, the potential for a collapse of the whole forest ecosystem is present. If this happens then much additional carbon dioxide would be released into the atmosphere, further adding to climate change.

None of these things needs to happen if sensible policies are adopted by governments, corporations, NGOs, and others. But policies to think carefully about what we are making within a changing biosphere are only beginning to be considered as climate change gets attention in many places. Clearly we are going to have to adapt to many changes but do so in ways that do not aggravate dangerous trends. The trick for policy now seems to be to recognize that we need to do adaptation and mitigation simultaneously, making sure that our adaptations mitigate tendencies that are disruptive, such as enhanced greenhouse gas production. When it comes to security the key point is that environmental change is upon us; it's the context in which we have to now think. But how we go about dealing with vulnerabilities and dangers caused by environmental change in the increasingly constructed contexts in which people live is key to rethinking security too. Environmental change requires us to rethink security in ecological terms. To do so requires combining the historical context of human affairs discussed in chapter 3 with the novel scientific understandings of the Anthropocene outlined in this chapter. In combining these matters we now have to understand both that we are making our own future in some important ways and that our increasingly artificial circumstances make us vulnerable in new ways too.

Thinking about security as requiring both simultaneously is now necessary if ecology and the changing biosphere are the taken-for-granted context for research and policy formulation. The term "Anthropocene" is significant because it captures in a single evocative word the new condition of humanity. The Anthropocene marks the new human condition in that we are actively remaking the ecological context of our times. This is not only a matter of atmospheric change, and of climate modifications as a result of the emissions from carboniferous capitalism, but also one of land-use changes, which continue to change the vegetation and animal life of the planet dramatically, pollution and fishing in the oceans, the introduction of new chemicals into all parts of the biosphere, and such things as the re-plumbing of most of the major rivers of the planet. Insecurity is now a matter both at the largest scale, in which we are changing the atmosphere and probably making extreme weather events more frequent, and also of the vulnerabilities manufactured by the artificial and urban land-scapes we increasingly live within.

5

Glurbanization and Vulnerability in the Anthropocene

The economic phenomena we talk about in terms of globalization are physical phenomena; global trade is moving stuff round the planet and turning rocks into air in ways that mean humanity has become a geomorphic and climatological agent, even if that is not quite what we think we are doing when we stop to fill our car's fuel tank on the way to the shopping mall to buy things made on the other side of the world. The sheer scale of human activity is novel, and we have begun a major transformation of the biosphere. If earth is the home of humanity then we are doing house renovations on a large scale without the help of an architect's plan, or any clear sense that there is a final point at which our remodeling will be finished, much less that all the modifications will fit together in a way that allows the structure to remain standing.

Humanity has been increasing in numbers, especially rapidly in the twentieth century. We are also moving from rural areas to urban ones and from farming as a dominant occupation to all sorts of other economic activities in towns and cities (Worldwatch Institute 2007). Even in apparently remote and poor areas of the world people are connected into the global economy. Entrepreneurs in the hills of Nepal rent their cell phones so farmers know the price of their produce in town before setting out on a long journey to sell their wares. Television sets bring news and football games to remote places; literally billions of people watch the World Cup games every four years. And they do so thanks to globe-spanning satellite technologies that bring images from stadiums into the poorest slums in the burgeoning cities of the global South. Many of those slums use the packing cases and boxes used to ship all manner of consumer goods, including the televisions to watch the World Cup around the planet, as building materials. We are becoming interconnected in ever more complicated ways as we reshape the biosphere.

Only recently have we become an urban species; in the first decade of the twenty-first century, for the first time in human history, the majority of us live in towns and cities, but we have moved into towns while linking these cities together in trade arrangements, tourism industry connections, and numerous long commodity chains that bring things from all over the world to the urban markets and the big box stores that purvey all manner of stuff. This is the network society that Manuel Castells (1996–8) described in the 1990s. The process is a matter of global urbanization, or what I term "glurbanization" in this chapter. We have moved to cities and connected up those cities in a global economy and communications system simultaneously; global cities are now nodes in an economy that links them in numerous ways in a complex assemblage (Sassen 2006). This is a new condition for humanity, one driven by the productive capabilities of industry and technology and the apparently insatiable demand for all sorts of consumer products in a global marketplace.

Earth-system science makes it clear that in glurbanizing the biosphere we have dramatically changed many of the basic parameters of human existence. All the movement of goods, raw materials, and people has introduced new physical and biological processes into the biosphere, changing many facets of how it behaves and probably increasing the risk of extreme weather events. But how these extreme events affect people depends on where they are, and how the social, economic, and physical infrastructure they depend on to stay alive is affected by the storms, droughts, fires, and other hazards that seem to be increasing in the Anthropocene.

It is important to understand this matter of vulnerability as a two-fold process. People's circumstances are increasingly artificial in the sense that they depend on technology, trade, and manufactured materials for food, water, shelter, and clothing. But they are also increasingly subject to storms, droughts, and other disruptions precisely because the technology, trade, and artificial places they live in at least indirectly disrupt weather systems. Thinking about vulnerability and the manner in which institutions provide safety and protection, the rationale for security in the first place, now requires that these new circumstances be worked into the thinking. Linking security with environmental change makes this new context of humanity the starting point for analysis (Brklacich and Bohle 2006).

History and prior experience may have much to teach us about hazards, vulnerabilities, and institutional responses in providing security in various forms, not only in terms of understanding hazards but also in thinking through how environment is understood as a threat, and how environmental phenomena are understood as something inevitable, the cause of many misfortunes, perhaps even the response of a seriously displeased deity. If disasters are constructed as natural, beyond the control of cultures, an act of God, as insurance companies term these things, then they are frequently deemed beyond human intervention. But insofar as people move into harm's way, living on marginal land vulnerable to floods, fires, and landslides in the slums of the burgeoning cities of the global South, and those floods, fires, and landslides are made more intense as a result of the anthropogenic disruptions, their vulnerability is increasingly artificial rather than in any way natural (Abramovitz 2001). Given that their means of subsistence is drawn mostly from commercial economic arrangements rather than more directly from subsistence agriculture, fishing, or hunting, then vulnerability is also about the operation of that economy, how economic policy, trading arrangements, and policy decisions about global agriculture are made in faraway places, or when local merchants hoard scarce supplies to inflate prices, very locally indeed.

Vulnerability

Human security is about freedom from harm, fear, and violence, but extending it to deal with environmental matters in cities, and in particular the slums of the South, is especially important if the concept is to have any meaning for the majority of humanity. Investigating insecurity requires understanding not only the social and economic dimensions of particular situations, but also the larger ecological context. But as this chapter makes clear, the ecological context is not a natural given set of circumstances. Crop failures in droughts may not be fatal to subsistence farmers, depending on the larger societal context and the availability of effective governance and relief arrangements. Preventing speculative price increases in the face of famine may allow for grain supplies to remain in areas where they are scarce, rather than being sent to where the price is higher as a result of speculation, as happened in the late Victorian holocausts. The global economy is tied to the ecological systems in complex ways; it is an increasingly large part of the biosphere; but the social arrangements and governance structures that construct the trade rules, profits, interest rates, and all the other conditions of marginal survival are key to determining who lives and who dies in particular circumstances.

Better precision is helpful in discussing such things, and here the literature dealing with natural hazards frequently focuses on the concept of vulnerability (Fussel 2007). More specifically, the classic formulation of vulnerability, in the discussion of natural hazards and threats that environmental change presents to people, emphasizes the "characteristics of a person or group in terms of their capacity to anticipate, cope with, resist and recover from the impact of a natural hazard" (Blaikie et al. 1995: 9). Obviously different people are more or less vulnerable depending on numerous social and economic factors. The focus in the analysis of hazards is usually on the most vulnerable, those most likely to have their lives, and crucially their livelihoods, most disrupted. Likewise there is a time dimension in this; those who take longest to recover their livelihood are most vulnerable. Livelihood refers to "the command an individual, family, or other social group has over an income and/or bundles of resources that can be used or exchanged to satisfy its needs. This may involve information, cultural knowledge, social networks, legal rights as well as tools, land, or other physical resources" (Blaikie et al. 1995: 9).

Geography matters in terms of vulnerability to hazards. Hillsides are vulnerable to landslides and severe rainfall, but a rich executive who buys a home on a hillside near Los Angeles to enjoy the view is not vulnerable in the same sense as a poor Brazilian or Filipino trader living in a hillside slum close to an urban market because he cannot afford to rent anywhere else. While the executive is likely to have warning of the weather event that threatens his house, even if his house is washed away despite engineering protections, he has insurance, credit, and an income, so he can rapidly re-establish his household. In contrast the trader's total stock of capital is probably the few possessions in his shack, and if these are washed away in a deluge, even if he has warning of the event and survives, he has no means to re-establish his livelihood. Thus while both may lose their homes the trader is much more vulnerable. In terms of human security policies, focusing on the most vulnerable both to try to limit their exposure to danger and to have strategies for helping them after a disaster is a priority.

This formulation of vulnerability relates to more or less discrete events and is loosely consistent with the second dimension of human security, described by the UNDP as "protection from sudden and hurtful disruptions in the patterns of daily life – whether in homes, in jobs or in communities" (UNDP 1994: 23). Vulnerability, in the natural hazard formulation, is less concerned with the formulation of human security in terms of "safety from such chronic threats as hunger, disease and repression" (UNDP 1994: 23). Nonetheless these dimensions of human security fit with the larger focus on a political economy approach to vulnerability, which deals with insecurities that are not so obviously dealt with directly by traditional national security means, but which are appropriate if people rather than states are the focus of security thinking (Liotta and Miskel 2008).

Focusing on entitlements and the social circumstances of particular people and organizations is also key to the broader political economy approach to vulnerability (Fussel 2007). Here the focus is not on the immediate events of a hazard, and a model of pressure and release, but the larger sets of circumstances in which the event happens. Given too that the UNDP (1994) formulation suggests that human security is threatened by amorphous changes, migration, and environmental factors, rather than by any deliberate hostile intent, the larger understanding of vulnerability is appropriately linked to human security. As the rest of this chapter suggests, humanity is increasingly vulnerable as a result of both the integration of much of the world into the global economy and the increasingly artificial circumstances in various built environments, which present direct hazards.

As such, much of the debate about vulnerabilities now focuses on "socio-ecological systems," in recognition that society and ecology are coupled and the contexts in which disasters happen are not just natural events but the unfolding of social and economic factors during and especially in the aftermath of the physical event (B. L. Turner et al. 2003). The disruption of environments may be of much less consequence than the aftermath where people's ability to cope is shaped by social factors. Some systems are much more resilient than others. Resilience is usually understood in terms of the ability of a system to bounce back from a disruption (Adger 2006). The larger the disruption that a system can rebound from the more resilient it is understood to be. Drawing on ecological understandings of systems resilience also refers to the ability of systems to self-organize and adapt to crises too, so that they may function once again after the disruption, but not necessarily in precisely the same way as they did before; in other words they may not revert to the prior state, but may nonetheless function in a new configuration as a result of their powers of rebuilding.

The last couple of decades have made matters of hazards, vulnerability, and human insecurity unavoidable as part of the discussion of environmental change and its security consequences. To draw on tabulations by the United Nations International Strategy for Disaster Reduction (2004: 2): in the 1990s notable events included Hurricane Mitch in 1998, which devastated much of the infrastructure of Central American states; the following year Mexico suffered floods that were more severe than any since 1600; a cyclone in India flattened 18,000 villages in 2000; the next year brought Hurricane Lingling, which killed 500 in South and East Asia. Huge floods hit Europe in the middle of 2002. A few years later the Strategy for Disaster Reduction (2007: 2) authors updated this list, noting that:

> The Bam earthquake of December 2003 in the Islamic Republic of Iran, the heat wave that affected Western Europe in 2003, the devastation caused by Hurricanes Ivan and Jeanne in Grenada and other Caribbean countries in September 2004, the Indian Ocean earthquake and tsunami in December 2004, Hurricane Katrina in the United States of America in August 2005 and the Kashmir earthquake of October 2005, accounted for more than 350,000 deaths and USD 194 billion of economic damage.

Clearly natural disasters are a major concern for any discussion of human security. They are matters of military policy, too, as frequently military forces are called upon to help with emergency shipments of supplies, portable hospitals, water supplies, evacuations, and many other tasks for which their logistics capabilities equip them (Foster 2005; Paul J. Smith 2007).

But perhaps even more significant in terms of long-term thinking about human security and environmental change is a pattern that emerges from the data when the mega-events, the disasters that kill large numbers of people, are taken out of the picture, and the frequency of smaller-scale disasters and their related casualties is considered. Here the trend over the last few decades shows a rise in the number of casualties, and in particular a clear trend in hazards caused by climatic events increasing faster than those caused by geologic events, and also faster than population growth (United Nations International Strategy for Disaster Reduction 2007). So, proportionally more people are vulnerable to events that can reasonably be assumed to be related to climate change. "Climate change in itself is perhaps the ultimate hazard. It not only magnifies existing patterns of disaster risk but is now producing dramatic changes to the planet's ecosystems, which in turn threaten the continued social and economic viability of entire regions" (United Nations International Strategy for Disaster Reduction 2007: 30).

In terms of policy responses, the literature on disasters sometimes discusses risk in terms of the hazard multiplied by the vulnerability, with risk highest where a serious hazard impacts the most vulnerable people. But in terms of responding to risk, the capabilities of institutions and people are frequently discussed in terms of capacity, understood as the strengths and resources of a society, people, or organization to reduce risk or respond to disaster (United Nations International Strategy for Disaster Reduction 2004). Capacity building may well enhance resilience; that is, the capabilities of societies and organizations to recover and bounce back after a disaster. Despite this rapidly growing discussion of hazards, policies for capacity building, vulnerability reduction, and resilience promotion, it is still noteworthy how little of the global change literature, and the climate-change discussions, have explicitly engaged the discussion of human security until fairly recently. In the emerging discussion of human security in cities the connections to natural hazards are not usually included (humansecurity-cities.org 2007). Focusing on harm and fear rather than environment has been the norm. Nonetheless new initiatives such as the United Nations University Institute for Environment and Human Security are beginning to develop these connections (Bogardi 2004; Brauch 2005a, 2005b).

Making these connections is important because the crucial point of the discussion of the Anthropocene, and the earth-system science's insistence that we are living in an increasingly artificial environment, is that the settings wherein humanity is insecure are artifacts of our own making. Admittedly many of them are not thought of in quite this light, but the vulnerabilities of numerous people to extreme events is mediated by numerous social and material realities. Thinking seriously about vulnerability now requires that the constructed, built environments in which we increasingly live and work be thought of in those terms explicitly. The absence of economic resources that renders rural populations vulnerable in times of drought has parallels in terms of contemporary urban vulnerabilities. This requires that we extend the thinking about disaster preparedness into the future, and insofar as lessons from the past can teach us about the future, then thinking intelligently about the context of death and destruction by extreme events may allow us to draw appropriate historical parallels for the new circumstances in the new "glurban" context of the imme-diate future for humanity.

Urban Vulnerabilities

Earthquakes suggest the changing context of our vulnerabilities; they offer some pointed lessons that need to be addressed by security planners. Buildings with seismic protection as part of their structures are far more likely to survive in the event of a tremor, and hence produce fewer casualties. Poorly designed structures, or ones that ignore building-code requirements for seismic upgrades, are most likely to collapse in the event of a quake, and collapsing buildings are what kill most victims of earthquakes. The total of 26,796 people killed in the Bam quake of December 2003 suggests that Iranians are far more likely to die in an earthquake than are either Japanese or

Americans, primarily because their context of vulnerability is so different (United Nations International Strategy for Disaster Reduction 2007: 13). Likewise gasoline pipelines, natural gas lines, and other inflammable infrastructure are a major hazard; although so long as supplies to the lines are promptly stopped damage can be minimized. Landslides that disrupt communications can seriously hamper relief efforts and poorly built dams may present further hazards too to those living downstream. In built environments vulnerability is linked to engineering, planning, and construction technologies, as well as the availability of relief capabilities (Pelling 2003).

So far in the first decade of the twenty-first century, a number of high-profile extreme events have taken a toll on populations in urban areas that highlight the fragility of the built environments that people live in. Hurricane Katrina in 2005 is an obvious example of this fragility. Inadequately maintained levees collapsed during the storm causing the flooding of New Orleans. The devastation that resulted shows that vulnerability is dependent to a very large degree on a combination of geography and infrastructure. Building a city under sea level requires a system of dikes and pumps to work in extreme circumstances. But the system failed precisely when it was needed most, with disastrous consequences for the poorest segment of the population who could not flee. While the hurricane killed many fewer than the Indian Ocean tsunami eight months earlier, Katrina's legacy remains a stark reminder of the vulnerabilities of contemporary coastal cities. The failure of the United States government to provide effective security before and after the hurricane forces us to consider the security priorities on the part of the Bush administration. Given the poor response by this administration to the city's large and vulnerable black population, it is not surprising that some commentators condemned the racism at the heart of the administration (Haider-Markel et al. 2007). The vulnerability of those without transport, epitomized by television pictures of desperate survivors clinging to rooftops as the flood waters swirled around them, brought home to many viewers the simple fact that disasters can strike anywhere.

These extreme events also posed questions about sea-level rise, increased intensity of hurricanes, and the role played by climate change. Even more significantly, the inadequate infrastructure of dikes and drainage canals was revealed. The significance of the dredging of channels for oil tankers and pipelines, the reduction of wetlands around the city, and the construction of a fabricated landscape with little buffering capacity to absorb floods also emerged as experts reconstructed the sequence of events (Freudenburg et al. 2007). Just as many communities had been rendered vulnerable to the tsunami's devastation at the end of 2004 by the removal of coastal mangroves that traditionally act as a protection against waves and storm surges, the artificial landscape of Louisiana offered little protection to the residents of New Orleans. The complexity of the administrative structure, and the lack of planning for emergency responders' communications, not to mention the vulnerability of their own families, compounded the difficulties of what was, not a little ironically, one of the most predicted disasters in history (Cigler 2007). It was the failure of the inadequately maintained drainage canals that were undermined by flooding that finally precipitated the worst inundation, which deprived many of the poor people of the city of their homes and livelihoods. Plans by the United States Corps of Engineers to upgrade the infrastructure had gone unfunded for years, despite repeated calls to shore up the dikes in a city that is slowly sinking ever further below sea level.

The examination of what went wrong in this case suggests the crucial importance of investigating the geography of who died, who subsequently became ill, and the multiple dimensions of their vulnerability. Looking at the photographs of the flood waters in New Orleans showing the survivors clinging to the rooftops in August 2005, and hearing of the increasing despair among the people in the Superdome, this author was reminded of a conversation he had at an international studies conference in New Orleans some years prior to Katrina. As frequently happens at these events the discussion turned to the advantages and disadvantages of the selected venue for the meeting. One conference participant said, "New Orleans is fine as a conference site this time of year, but there is no way I would come here during hurricane season!" "Why not?" I ventured. "Well, have you read the city evacuation plan?" he replied. I continued with a flippant rejoinder, which, in hindsight, I very much wish I had not made: "Ah, no, it's not part of my normal bedtime reading!" His final comment left me chilled: "Well, the evacuation plan says that the middle class get in their cars and drive away. The poor go to the Superdome and hope!"

The fact that nearly a quarter of a million mostly black residents of the city, in many cases the poor, the sick, and those without private automobiles, didn't have the option of leaving is a crucial part of the explanation, but other factors must be included too. If the city had declared a state of emergency earlier and mobilized buses to evacuate people, fewer casualties would have resulted. Looking back on the disaster and its aftermath, the conclusions are simple and clear:

> If we are to learn something from Katrina, it is that – in their circumstances and their resources – all people are not equal in the United States, and that there is both a geography and a social character to vulnerability. Living in New Orleans, living in certain neighborhoods of New Orleans, being African American, having limited income, being female, being a head of household, having young children in the home, suffering from chronic illnesses, and being pregnant can all contribute to vulnerability. As we drill down through these risks, it is easy to see how spatially and socially complex vulnerability is. It is not enough to map poverty; we have to understand the social dimensions within our maps. (Curtis et al. 2007: 327)

Lack of access to transport, or, if you had a car, of funds to buy gasoline, food, and accommodation if you left the city, was a large part of the story. So, too, were estimates that the storm would miss the city, and, as it turned out, misplaced faith in the dikes and pumping system.

But once the storm had passed, the canal banks gave way and flood water started to rise, it quickly became clear that planning to deal with what was happening simply wasn't adequate. International aid organizations found the lack of any coherent state response to the disaster made it seem as if they were working in the Third World rather than in a metropolitan state (Eikenberry et al. 2007). In the words of one commentator summarizing views from outside the United States: "The situation in New Orleans looked like an extremely underdeveloped African nation, hopelessly trying to get the attention of the world, and yet nothing was happening. This was an ugly picture the world took notice of; it was not just bad governance but 'ugly' governance"

(Farazmand 2007). The failure of the emergency planners then degenerated further into confusion when military units, and mercenaries from Blackwater corporation, were deployed apparently to protect the remaining property of the affluent from those dispossessed and in many cases in desperate need of assistance. This once again raises the question: security for whom?

Subsequently, the attempts to clean up the flood debris and begin reconstruction seemed to perpetuate the incompetence and inequities of the situation. While sports franchises and universities went to great lengths to reopen their establishments, the poor who had rented apartments in the city had no option but to wait to see if their landlords were going to either rehabilitate their apartment buildings or construct something new to which they could return. The poor had fewer opportunities to recover and reconstruct (Masozera et al. 2007). While not all structures were destroyed, nonetheless this vulnerability of non-property-owners is markedly more severe than that of those who could at least stake a claim to some real estate and attempt to initiate reconstruction (Green et al. 2007). In turn, those with resources had some claim on insurance and the disaster funds that flowed into the state, although most of those funds did not reach those who needed them most (Jurkiewicz 2007). Many people simply abandoned New Orleans and began new lives elsewhere; but nowhere was the discussion as to whether the city should even be rebuilt raised very seriously, despite the demonstrated vulnerability of the location and the obvious difficulties of preventing a repeat occurrence the next time a major hurricane bears down on the coast of Louisiana (Briggs 2006).

Heatwaves, Fires, and Floods

New Orleans is not the only place to suffer disaster as a result of extreme weather and inadequate infrastructure. Two summers prior to Katrina a heatwave in Europe caused numerous deaths in Paris, and elsewhere in cities in France in particular (Vandentorren et al. 2004). The elderly were especially vulnerable in apartments and housing that were not equipped to provide cooling. Heat, dehydration, and exhaustion took their toll on those unable to seek shelter elsewhere.

Once again the urban infrastructure was incapable of dealing with the situation. Massive forest fires are becoming more common in Greece, Portugal, California, and Australia too, fueled by intense, hot droughts that make fire seasons especially severe. That people build suburban housing developments in such circumstances is noteworthy, but once again vulnerability relates to the geography and the infrastructure and the simple fact that once huge fires get moving in these climates they are very difficult to stop. Looking at each of these examples in more detail provides some additional insights into vulnerability, who suffers where, and what might be done to prevent casualties.

The United Nations International Strategy for Disaster Reduction (2007: 30) quotes a figure of 34,947 deaths due to the heatwave in Western Europe in the summer of 2003, which in terms of deaths makes Katrina pale nearly into insignificance. But here, while the poor and elderly without access to cool accommodation were frequent victims, the physical infrastructure remained intact. While pictures of numerous coffins, and the resignation of some government ministers taking responsibility for the failure of medical services to offer timely interventions, did make the media coverage, the lack of whole-scale destruction and the absence of any apparent need to rebuild empha-size the point that hazards aren't equal; heatwaves are not destructive in the way that floods, hurricanes, and earthquakes are, although for the citizens of Paris, or Chicago in other summers, they may in fact be much more lethal.

In August 2006 forest fires forced the evacuation of tourists from coastal resorts in Greece. Fast-moving fires fanned by summer winds on top of drought conditions forced tourists from hotels onto beaches where they had to be evacuated by boat; the coast guard provided transport to take tourists off the beaches and to safety. This has become a pattern; Spain and Portugal have also had major fire events in recent years fueled by hot summer winds. In May 2008 the first tanker ship-ment of water to Barcelona arrived; the long-lasting drought there had finally forced the city to import water. Australians, too, find their cities endangered repeatedly by wild fires. California has had many major fire events in the aftermath of hot, dry summers recently. None of this should be surprising to anyone who looks at a world climate map. They are all in Mediterranean climate zones, and as all geography school students learn, that climate has cool, wet winters and hot, dry summers. But now it seems the summers are getting hotter and the fires that are part of the ecology of these zones are becoming more severe.

With people building luxury houses, tourist hotels, and apartments in areas prone to fires, it's perhaps not surprising that more severe events endanger people who have moved in. Presupposing that nature in these places behaves in a similar fashion to the more predictable patterns in North Europe or New England is an especially odd assumption, given that people go to Greece, California, and other Mediterranean climates precisely to escape cool, rainy places. But the assumption seems fairly persistent, leading Mike Davis (1999) to term the arguments that nature in California is perverse and hostile "the humid fallacy," because people think that the mild, wet climate of New England is in some sense "normal." Trying to suppress fires and demanding disaster assistance when they inevitably burn suggests a dangerous lack of awareness of the ecological context of vulnerabilities in these places. Insofar as environmental change is likely to increase the likelihood and severity of extreme events, then much more careful reflection on land-use decisions, building codes, and infrastructure provision in thinking about vulnerability and human security is clearly needed.

In late 2007 drought in the South East of the United States raised the alarming possibility of the city of Atlanta running out of water. Millions of citizens rely directly on the water supplies for drinking, cooking, and personal hygiene; the possibility of the taps running dry raises the specter of another mass evacuation in the South of the United States, this time due to a lack of water rather than the downpours and floods of Katrina. Part of the response is better cooperation between the states of the South East in agreeing to share what water is available in lakes and rivers; the other part will inevitably be the construction of new reservoirs to service the growing population in that part of the country. Once again infrastructure is key to understanding the vulnerability of the population to drought. But the United States has the resources to re-plumb the South East yet again, digging reservoirs, canals, introducing technological conservation measures, and pricing water sensibly to pay for these measures.

As humanity becomes an urban species billions of us are moving into the slums of the Southern cities. Urbanization of the poor in these huge centers frequently happens without careful planning or the provision of water, sanitation, drainage, and other essential urban services. The informal settlements of these cities are diverse, and generalizations about them need to be treated cautiously. They are dynamic social systems, complete with complicated modes of governance, even when formal state arrangements for water, electricity, and policing are absent. Nonetheless, where structures are built of scrap timber, packing cases, and whatever roofing materials can be scavenged in these rapidly growing cities, clearly they are not the robust structures of the formal sector of the economy. Those built on large river estuaries around ports or in large deltas are especially vulnerable to storms, flooding, and tsunamis.

The residents of Mumbai discovered just how vulnerable these are some weeks before those in New Orleans faced Katrina. In Mumbai in July 2005, torrential rains caused urban flooding of a different nature, washing away informal housing and killing hundreds of residents. More than 60 percent of the city was flooded as nearly a meter of rain fell in a couple of days. Unlike in New Orleans, where the rupture of key canals caused the flooding, the causes of Mumbai's difficulties were a complex combination of factors.

> Among them a few important are unplanned development of the city, reclamation of low lying areas, negligence on the part of Brihanmumbai Municipal Corporation (BMC) in cleaning sewers and drainages, builders' lobby encroaching the areas of hills and mangroves, irresponsible city dwellers' disregard for their streets, lanes and sewers, violation of coastal regulation zone (CRZ) rules, choking up of the Mithi river providing natural drainage to the city, lack of disaster preparedness, too many people migrating into the city, the presence of multiple administrative and development agencies like BMC, Mahanagar Telephone Nigam Limited, Mumbai Metropolitan Region Development Authority (MMRDA), Maharasthra Housing and Area Development Authority (MHADA), etc., with no clear coordination among them. (Bhagat et al. 2006: 338)

In addition to these difficulties, the fact that the emergency organizations themselves were hit by the flood, and apparently this eventuality wasn't considered in advance planning, combined with the lack of a communications system that allowed the authorities to communicate to coordinate their efforts, hampered efforts to cope. When floods cut rail links, knocked out electrical systems, and blocked roads, the cell-phone system, too, collapsed when the backup generators ran out of fuel and could not be resupplied. Fortunately, Mumbai, unlike New Orleans, was above sea level and the floods drained away in the weeks following the rain.

The larger causes of Mumbai's disaster are in many ways similar to the situation of New Orleans. The tendency toward heavier rainfall through the twentieth century and into the twenty-first is part of the story, but so too is the increased urbanization and the spread of concrete surfaces, which enhance runoff into drainage systems, many of which were at least partly clogged with debris and garbage. Wetlands, forested areas, and mangroves in the area have all been substantially reduced; as in New Orleans, the natural "sponges" in the area that can absorb rainfall have been diminished. Suburban Mumbai doesn't have a comprehensive drainage system, and it was here that some of the worst flooding took place (Gupta 2007). Numerous other infrastructure problems dealing with sewage and garbage also added to the difficulties the city faced. The many thousands of rotting carcasses of dead animals exacerbated the dangers of contamination. The transportation system that handles the millions of commuters couldn't cope with the floods either, forcing huge numbers of people to try to walk through flood waters to get home. Numerous businesses were brought to a standstill in the hub of India's economy.

Local responders, especially in the informal housing sectors, improvised as best they could. Commentators noted the numerous spontaneous acts of generosity that happened among strangers who did what they could to help stranded commuters and those flooded out of their basement or ground-floor apartments in the urban core.

> But what really captured the public imagination in the days
> following the floods were the selfless acts of young men
> conventionally seen by the middle classes as loafers, threatening
> the security of themselves and their families. In one area near
> one of the city's largest slums, young men, having been flooded
> out of their one-room shanties, spent the night swimming

through the raging water saving schoolchildren stranded
in school buses. Another group of boys made a rope and
carried hungry passengers to safety from the roof of a city bus.
(Anjaria 2006: 81)

Such acts changed the sociological assumptions of the elites, at
least temporarily:

Until now, researchers have only understood this mobile
population for its capacity for violence, but what July 26 revealed
was its capacity for incredible acts of generosity and selflessness.
And uncharacteristically, the upper classes acknowledged this
reality. Slum dwellers, who only days earlier had been declared
the greatest impediment to Mumbai achieving its global dreams,
were now declared to represent the "true spirit" of Mumbai.
(Anjaria 2006: 82)

Spontaneous actions by people filled at least some of the gaps
where public systems collapsed. No martial law was declared, and
while chaos reigned it wasn't marked by looting, riots, or the need
for troops. Mumbai's flooding in July of 2005 not only killed hundreds of citizens but, given the inability of the city infrastructure
and emergency systems to cope, changed the perspective of the elite
concerning the future of the city. Whereas before the flood the city
was heralded as India's financial center and a new global city set to
emulate Singapore or Shanghai, in the aftermath of the flood expec-
tations and investments were downgraded. Nonetheless innovations
have been set in motion, clogged drains cleared, emergency plans
arranged, and careful analysis of the city's hydrology is underway
to better prepare for future extreme rainfall. But it is clear that
while Mumbai's response, especially in the slums of the city, was
helped immensely by the informal community organizations, these
alone are not enough to rely upon in the face of future disasters (De
Sherbinin et al. 2007).

Many lessons have been learnt about what needs to be done; but
it remains to be seen if disaster planning will become widespread
elsewhere, especially in low-lying coastal areas. But one political
lesson is that populations have a great capacity for self-help in dangerous circumstances. Those scholars who studied the outpouring

of assistance by church groups and numerous other organizations helping migrants from New Orleans observed that these activities were frequently overlooked by the US media, because its security script focused on threatening mobs and military intervention. It's in this outpouring of assistance and the donations by people far and wide to disaster aid and help in rebuilding that hope lies, and the possibilities of much more constructive security policy too.

Securitizing the Victims: Imperial Vision Once Again

As if the combination of years of neglect of America's urban cores, coupled to an incompetent response to Hurricane Katrina, weren't bad enough, many commentators were alarmed by the statements made by Bush administration officials. Stephen Graham (2006) argues that the administration had frequently derided poor people as moral failures and denigrated what it portrayed as cultures of welfare dependency in the cities. While the affluent of New Orleans had been able to get in their cars and drive to safety when the evacuation order was given, the poor had remained behind. Graham (2006) summarizes the Bush administration response:

> Michael Chertoff, Bush's Secretary of Homeland Security, made a striking remark. Defending his administration's decision to basically abandon those who failed to leave using their own transport to their own devices, and ignoring the fact that most poor residents stayed because they simply had *no means to escape*, Chertoff argued that "the critical thing was to get people out of [New Orleans] before the disaster. Some people chose not to obey that order. That was a mistake on their part."
>
> Such rhetoric, backed by an almost complete absence of organized, public evacuation procedures, suggested one simple but powerful thing: if you can't get out of the city (like rich, suburban, auto owners) it's your fault. End of story. The escapees are normal, respectful, citizens. You're not. The social Darwinist, individualist and deeply anti-urban ideology that underpins so much of Bush's neoconservative world-view is rarely revealed so succinctly.

Henry Giroux (2006: 175) made a similar point in slightly different terms:

> The Bush administration was not simply unprepared for
> Hurricane Katrina as it denied that the federal government alone
> had the resources to address catastrophic events; it actually
> felt no responsibility for the lives of poor blacks and others
> marginalized by poverty and relegated to the outskirts of society.
> Increasingly, the role of the state seems to be about engendering
> the financial rewards and privileges of only some members of
> society, while the welfare of those marginalized by race and class
> is now viewed with criminal contempt.

Giroux (2006) analyzes the language used by the authorities to mar-
ginalize the victims of the flood, and specifically their construction
as a threat to the social order of affluence. As the failure of the rescue
mission became abundantly clear, the role of the military became
a central theme in how events were reported. The dominant script
changed from disaster to threat, and in the process much of what was
actually happening, the frantic efforts to offer assistance by numerous
groups and organizations, the spontaneous actions of people with
boats to help those stranded on rooftops, became less important.

A few reported episodes of guns being discharged, and some uncor-
roborated reports of rape in the media, rapidly focused the attention
of first responders on violence rather than on rescue. Racial and
sexualized fears of black men appeared in the script of the event and
distracted attention from needs for assistance. Disasters in Baghdad
suddenly looked very like those in the Bayou (Gelinas 2007). Both
are security problems first and foremost; both apparently required
military interventions:

> Within a few days after Katrina struck, New Orleans was under
> martial law occupied by nearly 65,000 U.S. military personnel.
> Cries of desperation and help were quickly redefined as the pleas
> of "refugees," a designation that suggested an alien population
> lacking both citizenship and legal rights had inhabited the Gulf
> Coast. Images of thousands of desperate and poor blacks gave way
> to pictures of combat-ready troops and soldiers with mounted
> bayonets canvassing houses in order to remove stranded civilians.

> Embedded journalists now travelled with soldiers on Humvees,
> armored carriers, and military helicopters in downtown USA.
> What had begun as a botched rescue operation by the federal
> government was transformed into a military operation. Given the
> government's propensity to view those who are poor and black
> with contempt, it was not surprising that the transformation of
> New Orleans and the Gulf Coast from disaster area to war zone
> occurred without any audible dissent from either the general
> public or the dominant media. New Orleans increasingly came
> to look like a city in Iraq as scores of private soldiers appeared on
> the scene – either on contract with the Department of Homeland
> Security or hired by wealthy elites to protect their private estates
> and businesses. (Giroux 2006: 176)

In terms of how this whole situation is understood as a matter of security, what quickly became clear is that the poor and the marginal were the threat to be controlled. Reduced to victims and refugees, their citizenship and many claims to be political agents in the situation were effectively removed. Here the state acted against its own population, or at least that section of it that has not been effectively included in the consumer society. Poverty and marginalization become, in Giroux's (2006) cutting phrase, "the biopolitics of disposability."

But Giroux's comment about the lack of audible dissent is not the whole story, as numerous critics of the neo-conservative policies have subsequently noted (Klein 2007). A major debate has followed about the politics of disasters, but one from which very different political lessons are drawn. Theologian Rosemary Radford Ruether (2006: 181) summarizes matters succinctly:

> Thus the responses to Katrina are reflecting a divergence of two
> worlds of thought and social conscience in this country. One,
> forwarded by the Federal government and big business, seeks to
> ignore the message revealed by the disasters in terms of poverty,
> racism and environmental degradation and continue with more
> of the same. A divergent view seeks to really learn from these
> lessons and shape plans for the future that would avert or at least
> lessen such disasters in the future. Unfortunately those pushing
> the first view have much more power and wealth than those
> seeking the second.

Rarely have the politics of security been more obvious. The neo-conservative view in Washington dismisses the lot of the poor and seems oblivious of the need to change security priorities. A wide range of other perspectives is beginning to understand the need to rethink disasters, and the vulnerabilities of people in artificial environments that render them vulnerable to hazards that are increasingly "unnatural" (Abramovitz 2001).

This event has ominous implications for other situations of urban vulnerability if such specifications of danger become the normal operating framework for state interventions in emergencies elsewhere (Graham 2009). The politics of security are rarely more obviously visible than in this crude and heavy-handed attempt to reassert the power of the state in the aftermath of an episode that had revealed its complete lack of concern for the fate of its poorest citizens. While it might be objected that Giroux's (2006) angry polemic is overstated, his trenchant prose does pose the crucial question of whose security is at stake in this episode more clearly than most. It raises the crucial point about an imperial view of the vulnerable and displaced as a threat first and foremost, and as citizens entitled to a say in how their lives are to be reassembled only secondarily, if at all.

It's the same attitude of disregard for the practicalities of the lives of the poor that was shown in the nineteenth century in India and elsewhere by imperial administrators, who, convinced that the operation of the market was the most important principle, ignored the fate of the starving people in their charge (Davis 2001). Constructing the dispossessed and starving as a threat to imperial rule, they understood the operation of their power as primarily about maintaining control of political order, not about aiding the population in need. In short, what was securitized was the administrative apparatus and the market; threats to these are paramount. If ensuring the survival of these institutions by the use of force means that poor people die in the process, that is apparently unfortunate, but not a matter of great concern so long as the imperial administration remains intact. And if a stingy, angry, or dangerous external nature can be blamed for the misfortunes of the marginal, in this logic, so much the better.

Anthropocene Security 2

But the examination of matters in terms of both globalization and earth-system science makes this argument much more difficult to sustain, precisely because those marginal people cannot now be presented as such so easily. Precisely because of the dislocations of globalization and the interconnections of the global economy on the one hand, and the disruptions of ecosystems on the other, it is now much more difficult to present the victims of disasters as entirely the makers of their own fate, or disconnected from the moral and economic obligations of the larger world community. Even more than this, the disruptions of climate change make it clear that vulnerability is not only a matter of being in harm's way, but also a matter of hazards aggravated by the disruptions of the biosphere insofar as those disruptions make droughts or storms more severe or more frequent. But disruptions of the food-supply system and communications systems too that feed the urban population are now part of security.

All of these considerations apply in relation to disaster, when preparations beforehand, and reactions in the early days afterwards, matter greatly to affected people. While disasters might not apparently be understood as being part of environmental change, and hence not appropriate matters for consideration in a discussion of policy and peacebuilding, the old joke about disasters simply being fast environmental change, and environmental change being slow disasters, suggests a direct relevance precisely because the vector of change is usually some form of "natural" phenomenon. Wars and political instabilities are forms of disaster too, but the disruptions of the biosphere, of which climate change is only the most high-profile, suggest that storms and vulnerabilities due to people living in places subject to the ravages of "natural" events are increasingly a matter of artificial environments, in which vulnerability due to social and political phenomena plays out. In a world of lengthy food chains, possibly more severe hurricanes (Shepherd and Knutson 2007), and climate change, the human context is increasingly artificial. This is the point about understanding ourselves as living in a new geological era called the Anthropocene. What is not yet clear in many discussions is that the Anthropocene might also be understood as the physical manifestations of globalization, a phenomenon that is about using fossil fuels as energy to move huge quantities of material quite as much as it is about moving money or changing identities.

Globalization is a matter of constructing new urban spaces, ones where the majority of humanity now live. It is a physical process of environmental change that unavoidably challenges the conventional thinking about security (Brauch et al. 2008). Vulnerabilities and the possibilities of either cooperation and peacebuilding or conflict and violence play out in these increasingly artificial landscapes. While peacebuilding and environmental matters are usually understood in terms of rural matters and usually among the marginal populations of the global South, the Anthropocene suggests that, as we become an urban species, the disruptions we have set in motion on the large scale will play out in the artificial landscapes of our "Planet of Slums," to borrow Mike Davis' (2006) provocative formulation. But whether these slums are portrayed as the source of threats to the neo-liberal economic progress of the future that require security policies to contain, or are seen as thriving human communities whose lot in life can be aided, and for whom timely infrastructure provision will be needed to help them survive climate disruptions, matters greatly in terms of how peacebuilding might now proceed and how human vulnerabilities are changing in increasingly artificial circumstances.

But in all this discussion it is important to remember J. K. Mitchell's (2006) insistence on seeing cities as complex entities, more than simply the sum total of vulnerabilities. The contrast between Mumbai and New Orleans has made some of this clear. But cities are more than their infrastructure too, however important pumps, drainage systems, water supplies, cell-phone towers, and bridges may be. They are also centers of innovation, in which populations have the ability to learn and change drastically, as the Mumbai experience shows. In this sense metaphors of organisms may be much more helpful than ones of cities as regulated territories. So, too, understanding cities as performance spaces may help; clearly who performed what roles in the dramas of Mumbai's and New Orleans' floods is key to understanding the very different responses. If we think in these terms, one of the key lessons for security is the capability of people to innovate and perform in productive ways outside the official script. Both the

Mumbai flood and the efforts by NGOs in New Orleans also suggest the importance of social networks and their speedy invention in the face of disaster; security planning can learn valuable lessons here for facilitating adaptation and building resilience into human systems to prevent "unnatural hazards" turning into disasters.

6

Geopolitics and Ecological Security

In the new circumstances of urban life in the Anthropocene, how might we now think about security? What kind of human institutions are needed to facilitate living well in changing times? How now might our notions of development and economics, the role of public institutions, and the ethical obligations we have to each other and to future generations be rethought in light of the new context of human life? These are huge questions, but necessary ones if the history, science, and new context for humanity are to be taken seriously in both academic investigations and political action. Clearly we are making our collective future, whether intentionally or not. So too how we collectively respond to disruptions, migrations, and insecurities in the future matters. None of these concerns seems to have very much to do with the geopolitical formulation of security that comes from the Cold War period; security really does need to be thought of differently now that we are beginning to understand the new context of the Anthropocene.

In all this, as the comparison of New Orleans and Mumbai makes clear, how security is articulated in a crisis is crucial. If the poor are portrayed as a threat to the prosperous, and military institutions are used to deal with these "threats," then violence, boundary fences, and conflict are likely. If, however, a broader understanding of security is invoked, one that recognizes the interconnectedness of humanity and the vulnerabilities of many people due to the increasingly artificial circumstances in which we live, then the possibilities for less violent and more constructive responses open up. International aid, NGO assistance, and cooperation in the face of disasters are becoming standard in international thinking; the very fact that the United Nations has taken substantial initiatives for prevention of disasters is encouraging. What kind of security is invoked is crucial because it justifies building specific types of institutions to cope with future disruptions. Portraying environmental refugees as a threat suggests the need for border fences, immigration controls, and military preparations to "secure" borders. Understanding them as in need of assistance suggests focusing on disaster preparations, aid agencies, and preparing to facilitate migration.

In this chapter as in chapter 5, the contrast between human security and traditional military security is rather starkly drawn. This re-emphasizes a major theme through this book about the importance of focusing on who and what is portrayed as a threat, and how security is invoked to deal with what is portrayed as a threat to which political order. Security cannot be separated from the geopolitical specification of the world that is frequently implicit in these formulations. Insofar as security is understood as a matter of protecting spaces from threats that are understood as external, a matter of spatial exclusion, or "keeping the bad guys out," then it attributes causality to foreign forces, and mandates a forceful response to "secure" the domestic polity from external predations.

But as the discussions of environmental history in chapter 3 and ecological science in chapter 4 make clear, this geopolitical specification of danger is no longer tenable. The ecological interconnections across frontiers, and the changes wrought on distant places by the practices of ecological imperialism, are the causes of many disruptions. The expansion of these patterns into a fully globalized economy, which, by its mode of carboniferous capitalism, is changing the biosphere to such an extent that we now live in a new geological period, the Anthropocene, logically precludes using such a geopolitical formulation of security.

> The distribution of current emissions points to an inverse relationship between climate change risk and responsibility. The world's poorest people walk the Earth with a very light carbon footprint. We estimate the carbon footprint of the poorest 1 billion people on the planet at around 3 percent of the world's total footprint. Living in vulnerable rural areas and urban slums, the poorest billion people are highly exposed to climate change threats for which they carry negligible responsibility. (UNDP 2007: 43)

This point is now unavoidable, but it does raise difficult matters of how humanity's condition is to be appropriately mapped, and who has responsibility in a world where national frontiers cannot be taken as the given categories for political action (Vanderheiden 2008). That of course won't stop political elites invoking nationalism and the defense of the realm in a crisis; such is the logic of securitization. But it does make it clear that such strategies are now based on a completely inappropriate geography for dealing with the causes of disruptions. They simply reassert control to handle some of the symptoms, or discuss interventions to deal with obvious and short-term disruptions, rather than dealing with the root causes. They focus only on adaptation to climate change rather than mitigating its causes.

The formulation of human security in 1994 by the UNDP recognized the crucial importance of the unintended cross-frontier causes of insecurity. Nonetheless the formulation of a geopolitics of external danger requiring metropolitan interventions frequently remains in this discussion, especially in the extension of the human security agenda to deal with humanitarian disasters, and the formulation of a "responsibility to protect" within the framework of state sovereignty in the work of the International Commission on Intervention and State Sovereignty (ICISS 2001). Linking security to ecology, rather than to traditional formulations of environment understood as something external that "we" need to manage, is a necessary corrective to this mode of thinking, albeit not a corrective that necessarily provides a straightforward policy agenda.

The rest of this chapter teases out these themes, turning first to some recent extensions of the notion of human security and then to the discussion of the ICISS framework and to Robyn Eckersley's (2007) extension of the framework to deal with environmental emergencies. In doing so the chapter further extends the argument about who should act, and how, if ecological formulations are taken seriously as the basis for a security policy in the Anthropocene. The contrast with some more traditional military interpretations of security and the potential for conflict, should migrants and environmental refugees be designated as threats, emphasizes once again the importance of focusing on the implications of which geopolitical framework is invoked in a crisis.

Extending Human Security

In contrast to the military focus, and the assumptions that national borders have to be secured in a crisis even at the cost of many lives of would-be migrants, the human security focus shifts attention from states to people, and to the circumstances that make them vulnerable in the first place. Rather than putting states, or war, or disease, or environment at the center of the analysis, as traditional international relations scholarship does, the human security discussion makes people the focus (Goucha and Crowley 2008). By focusing on people's vulnerabilities and what makes them insecure in the first place, attention is drawn to their context and where they are situated in the flow of artificial and natural energies and materials. Such considerations raise a host of issues for scholars of security policies. While there clearly is a role for a military dimension in disaster relief, the traditional understandings of national security and the priority given by states to military preparations have little to offer by way of guidance as to policy and preparations for dealing with increased hazards and disasters accentuated by environmental changes that are looming in the coming decades. If traditional policy responses emphasize migrants and disaster victims as a threat to national security, and as an external disruption that must be contained, then the fate of those subject to environmental disruptions may simply become worse (Paul J. Smith 2007).

If, however, disaster politics works to encourage international cooperation and humanitarian assistance, then new habits of collaboration may change security policies quite dramatically. The point is that states and, especially, NGOs are frequently motivated to assist across national borders when disaster strikes. How they do so matters, and the disaster research clearly suggests that enhancing resilience is important, as is post-disaster reconstruction. But who decides on what is reconstructed and how matters too; the ability of dynamic commercial sectors to take advantage of the destruction brought by disasters, and to do so at the cost of the more vulnerable parts of society, is a long-established pattern (Klein 2007). In this the experience of the poor in the ninth ward of New Orleans is broadly similar to those in part of the Indian Ocean in the aftermath of the tsunami there, where elites moved to reconstruct tourist hotels while removing poor fishing families from beach areas – for their own safety, of course.

Broadening security to include such considerations – and the United Nations formulation of human security in the 1994 UNDP does just this – requires a much more complicated formulation of security than is present in traditional international relations. This new, broadened agenda requires consideration of security for whom, from what threats, and provided how in what specific circumstances. Vulnerability analysis makes it clear that simple invocations of society are not enough to formulate policy; clearly gender, age, social circumstances, and wealth all matter in how insecurity happens (Neumayer and Plumper 2007). In trying to respond to this problematique, Ursula Oswald Spring (2008) has suggested a conceptualization in terms of "human, gender and environmental security" (HUGE). While HUGE is certainly a very apt acronym for this agenda, the necessity to try to think all the facets of human insecurity together is now unavoidable where vulnerability is taken seriously (Oswald Spring et al. 2009).

Oswald Spring's (2008) formulation of gender extends it beyond a simple male-and-female dichotomy to suggest that gender is key to a more complicated sociological imagination that includes children, elders, indigenous peoples, and other minorities as agents in the human dimensions of environmental challenges, in the need for peacebuilding in numerous places, and in attempts to tackle equity issues. Gender understood in these terms connects with security understood in terms of livelihood, food, health, education, public safety, and cultural diversity. This challenges hierarchies and violence that have made so many vulnerable by the way gender roles have shaped societies, and suggests very clearly that human security has to focus on these people rather than on maintaining the social order that simply perpetuates the control and safety of rich men running states.

HUGE thus also looks to other social organizations, equity, and development, and such things as ethical investment strategies, and broad public participation in political decision-making to tackle discrimination and violence, to secure humanity. Consequently "environmental security" concerns are incorporated because a healthy environment and strategies of resilience-building for vulnerable groups, and especially for women, should reduce the impacts of hazards. To do so, especially in areas that are hazard prone, this approach focuses on both the potential for financial and technical innovations that enhance women's own resilience from the bottom up, and the provision of state institutions that can warn of impending hazards, organize evacuations, and facilitate relief and reconstruction efforts subsequently. Advance planning to deal with disasters in isolated regions might help greatly to prevent famine or violent conflict in their aftermath. But to do all this requires both an understanding of the complexity of human networks and support systems and a political commitment to aid all citizens facing hazards. It also requires a recognition of the increasingly interconnected social and ecological systems that are the contemporary human context. Finally it requires making resources available to plan for contingencies, and this is especially difficult in developing countries where state capacity is limited and recent development priorities have been about the private sector and the supposed superiority of the market to provide for people's needs.

A similar set of concerns structures Hans Günter Brauch's (2005b) formulation of matters in terms of human and environmental security and peace (HESP), explicitly linking together the environmental and structural factors that render people insecure with an orientation to international institutions and peacebuilding. This is an attempt both to develop a research agenda and orient it to the particular circumstances that make people insecure, and to promote a policy agenda that takes this orientation seriously. Much conceptual work needs to be done to link environmental change with specific regional outcomes, and to link the key themes of sustainable development with sustainable peacebuilding and simultaneously with a reconceptualized theme of security; nor are narrow scientific studies necessarily helpful if they abstract technical issues from the larger human context of vulnerability.

These ideas link directly to what Brauch has called a new pillar of human security in terms of "freedom from hazard impacts." Building on earlier formulations of human security, in particular in terms of the themes of the freedom from fear and freedom from want, promoted by the Human Security Network and the Human Security Center (2005) and the Commission on Human Security (2003) respectively, Brauch (2005a) has suggested a "freedom from hazards" policy approach. This is loosely similar to the focus in HUGE emphasizing the importance of building resilience and dealing promptly with disaster impacts. Consistent with the original UNDP orientation, its focus is on preventing and anticipating dangers rather than on reactions after the event. As such it links directly to international disaster prevention initiatives and emergency policy measures. It does so with an explicit recognition of the growing dangers of global environmental change and the need to think about infrastructure provision and international cooperative efforts. All of which suggests a very different view of security from a reactive one of using the troops to prevent disruptions to social order after "nature" has done her worst.

Interventions, Ecology and the Responsibility to Protect

Nonetheless there obviously will be times when forms of intervention for emergency assistance are needed. There might also be times and circumstances where intervening to prevent an environmental disaster is necessary. But where and when and who legitimizes which invocation of security to justify such interventions goes to the heart of the matter of the geopolitical specification of environmental danger. This thinking about the international dimensions of human security, and the obligations on the part of states and the international community to protect citizens of all states from security threats, links up with the discussion of human security in terms of the appropriate response to humanitarian emergencies and what has become known, following the title of the 2001 ICISS report, as *The Responsibility to Protect*. This formulation, subsequently adopted by many members of the United Nations, suggests that states have the obligation to provide for the safety of their citizens, and should they very obviously fail in this duty the international community has the responsibility to intervene to provide the necessary assistance. The human security theme is key; people are the referent object, not states. This isn't national security understood in traditional terms of protecting borders; it's about human survival and the institutions to ensure this.

While this leads to all sorts of policy dilemmas in particular situations (Weiss 2007), it is especially fraught when it comes to discussions of interventions in other states, not least the suggestions in May 2008 that the international community ought to use force to ensure that the government of Myanmar distributed aid to the victims of Cyclone Nargis. The "responsibility to protect" principle might be read as an attempt to reinvent the type of social contract between peoples and rulers that was apparently demolished in many places by the expansion of carboniferous capitalism and nineteenth-century imperialism. Where, as discussed in chapter 3, the eighteenth-century Qing dynasty understood its obligations to take measures to ensure the survival of its people, the twenty-first-century arguments about the responsibility to protect suggest similar obligations.

In the face of environmental change and the possibilities of extreme events, aggravated ENSO events, or other disruptions, then, what are the responsibilities of states to protect their peoples? In part this requires a prior question concerning who is most likely to be affected by environmental change. Clearly, impoverished subsistence farmers are at high risk from the combination of matters in political ecology. So too are the slum dwellers in many of the informal settlements of the cities of the South. Rising sea levels and hurricanes render marginal peoples in the South especially vulnerable, but those in the "north of the north" round the Arctic circle too have already had their lives disrupted by climate change (Dalby 2003). Who might intervene where and how to deal with these human insecurities?

While humanitarian intervention is highly controversial in a system where sovereignty has long been the principle on which the United Nations system at least notionally operates (Jackson 2000), the theme of the necessity to intervene in a crisis where a state is incapable is now part of the larger human security agenda, and it reflects in part the larger shift toward cosmopolitan sensibilities that globalization has initiated. The arguments for intervention are heavily circumscribed to deal with the obvious objections to the violation of national sovereignty (Bain 2001). Both pressing urgency and serious consequences are necessary to justify an intervention; the principle is clearly an extraordinary measure to be invoked in times of complex humanitarian emergency, rather than as a matter of the routine operation of international relations. At its heart the human security agenda sets up a clash of norms, between the traditional one of non-intervention and the obligations to help across those frontiers (Hampson et al. 2002).

Nonetheless it is important to emphasize that the logic of intervention is also close to the thinking which became part of the framework for the Bush administration's "war on terror," with its specification of the world as in need of interventions of various kinds to finally integrate the world economy and eliminate tyranny (Dalby 2007b), and where ungoverned spaces and failed states too provide the logic for forcible intervention because of the threats that supposedly emanate from there (Galgano 2006). In these circumstances it is not at all surprising that states facing disasters are highly suspicious of calls for intervention on the part of Western states. Nonetheless, given the extirpation of species, the damage done by numerous industrial accidents, and the spill-over effects of many environmental and economic phenomena in a world that is now much more connected, questions of who might intervene where and when persist, and will no doubt become more intense in coming years as "environmental" crises mount. Despite the dismissal of proposals for "green helmets" in the 1980s and subsequent discussions in the 1990s (Dabelko 2008), the question of intervention and of the implicit allocations of blame and responsibility for dealing with environmental difficulties persists.

Robyn Eckersley (2007) has undertaken an ambitious attempt to extend the humanitarian intervention debate into matters of when and where there might be a right to intervention in the face of a major environmental disaster. In trying to extend the ICISS framework she suggests that intervention justification requires that there be a short-term extreme environmental emergency, one serious enough to overcome the norm of sovereignty and non-intervention, and the capability to mount such an intervention on the part of some external powers. She also makes it clear that such interventions only make sense when there has been a clear failure, either through lack of capacity or sheer unwillingness on the part of the state, to deal with the situation. Her analysis focuses in on two hypothetical possibilities: first, an imminent nuclear reactor meltdown accident, a repeat of Chernobyl in 1986, where a government fails to do what is necessary to prevent an accident; and second, the extinction of the great apes in

Rwanda, a species that she argues is a key part of the biological heritage of the planet and hence worthy of survival.

Eckersley's elegant and eloquent argument concerning the limits of "ecological intervention" is constrained by the scope of what is included in her definition of environmental emergency, by what might be in need of protection, and also by what is conventionally understood by notions of intervention related to states and sovereign territory. Her exploration of the limits of intervention as conventionally understood raises, in an especially pointed way, the related questions of who can legitimately intervene, where, and in what circumstances, and the matter of who it is that might be capable of actually doing those interventions. As such, her contribution to the debate is a most useful extension of the discussion of the ICISS framework not least because it highlights the ethical dilemmas, but also precisely because it explicates the limits of the framework itself.

Quite why the international community might intervene in a case such as the threatened eradication of the great apes in Rwanda, as she suggests, when it failed to intervene to save thousands of Rwandans in 1994 isn't so clear. But taking the argument seriously suggests that many of those in the "South" whose lives and, in the case of low-lying island states, even the existence of their states are in jeopardy, as a result of climate change caused mostly by Northern consumption, have a much better justification for intervening in the North to stop the profligate consumption of fossil fuels that threaten them than those Northerners have for intervening in the South on whatever "environmental" grounds. Except of course those marginal, poor Southern peoples who are most vulnerable to the storms and disruptions aggravated by climate changes don't have the military capabilities for intervention to prevent the disruptions of their societies. The best they can hope for is that the North will finally live up to some of its obligations to supply aid in compensation for Southern states joining international conventions to deal with problems they didn't create but of which, regardless, they will have to suffer the consequences (Roberts and Parks 2007).

While Eckersley's (2007) case is clear and to the point, the larger questions hanging over this discussion relate both to harms that cross borders and to the agents empowered to act to prevent these harms.

The arguments that Daniel Deudney (1990, 1998, 1999a) made back in the 1990s implied that taking environmentalism seriously required rethinking the assumptions of the state system as an effective provider of an ecologically sustainable future. The 1990s literature on human security, with its important point that people are frequently endangered by the unintended consequences of actions undertaken without hostile intent, is an important precursor to the "responsibility to protect" principle. These unintended consequences are not necessarily what Eckersley (2007) suggests would fit the criteria of immediacy that could, she argues, justify intervention on the basis of the right to "ecological defense." But if they endanger people in particular places, is some mode of defense justifiable? Might there be other modes of intervention by actors other than the military?

Anthropocene Interventions?

Where Eckersley (2007) draws attention to fairly narrow terrestrial environmental phenomena and poses the question of interventions to deal with these matters, the larger environmental "emergency" that we collectively face is not obviously amenable to interventions of the sort she discusses. The argument through this book suggests that taking ecology seriously as a science requires a larger and more encompassing view of what might be in need of ecological defense. In the last couple of decades, as chapter 4 has discussed, science has made dramatic strides in understanding the biosphere and the dynamics of planetary systems. Earth-system sciences have made clear that humanity and the rest of the biosphere are interlinked much more closely than the normal assumptions of life in territorial states suggest. This science has also suggested that the most important drivers of the biosphere are in many ways not terrestrial, but the atmosphere and the oceanic system, which between them determine the climatological conditions for land-based species. The most important mechanisms shaping our biosphere are oceanic and atmospheric systems that we are actively altering in the Anthropocene.

The important point is that the international system of states, granted responsibility for ensuring protection to its peoples, can be judged to have fairly systematically failed to act in a prudent manner to head off the worst imminent effects of these changes. The Kyoto protocol, for all its faults, is an international agreement under which some states have obligations to reduce their carbon emissions. Failure to live up to these obligations is fairly directly leading to changes that will, in the foreseeable future, have consequences for the territorial integrity of many states and even the physical survival of a few. While this may, as Eckersley (2007) argues, be a more gradual process than a nuclear reactor meltdown, or perhaps, although this is really unlikely, a more reversible process than the elimination of a species closely similar to humans, as in her Rwandan ape example, the sheer scale of the changes in the biosphere, and its fundamental challenge to the survival of low-lying atoll states in the Indian and Pacific oceans in particular (Barnett 2005), are surely a much more compelling case for emergency action to prevent their inundation and elimination as states and peoples.

The atoll states in the Pacific and Indian oceans and the low-lying littoral states, in particular Bangladesh (Karim and Minura 2008) and, as tropical storm Nargis in 2008 showed, Myanmar, which are especially vulnerable to storms, have no military options to intervene in this threat to their physical survival, now knowingly exacerbated by the affluent states, the annex I countries under the Kyoto protocol, which disregard their international commitments. What then is to be done, and by whom? How might a responsibility to protect be acted upon by the poor and marginal states in response? Those directly subject to sea-level rise, the possibility of more severe hurricanes, and other possible hydro-meteorological hazards surely have a compelling ethical argument for recourse to "ecological defense" in the face of the profligate use of fossil fuels in developed states, which indirectly, and probably unintentionally, endangers their populations and territory.

For the purposes of comparison with Eckersley's two examples, let us consider a future scenario involving Canada. It is apposite to use a Canadian example both because this book was written in Ottawa, the same city where the ICISS report formulating the responsibility to protect was drafted, and because, as the UNDP (2007: 10) pointedly notes in its *Human Development Report* on fighting climate change,

Canada is one of the worst offenders in violating its Kyoto emission commitments. At least as of 2009 it seems unlikely that Canada will try to use either drastic curbs on energy production or international carbon-trading mechanisms to attempt to in some way offset its profligate ways. Hence the following scenario.

Sometime in the next few years, after facing inundations by storm surges aggravated by rising sea levels, members of the Alliance of Small Island States (AOSIS) meet in an emergency conference to ponder what might be done. AOSIS passes a motion invoking the collective right of its members to ecological defense. While obviously all fossil fuels are a problem, the delegates decide that they should act against one of the worst sources of the threats to their ecological and territorial integrity. The preamble to the motion notes that Canada is not the only state in violation of its Kyoto commitments, but that it is on a per capita basis among the worst offenders. The motion goes on to explain that the continued exploitation of the huge tar sands deposits in Alberta, which require large amounts of energy just to extract petroleum before it even gets used, is an especially wasteful use of fossil fuels (Marsden 2007). Finally the AOSIS motion points out that subsidies and policies favoring the resource sector in Canada persist while relatively few innovations have been made to either improve efficiencies or expand renewable energy supplies (Jeffrey Simpson et al. 2007). Harkening back to the early 1990s debate about the key distinction between survival and luxury uses of energy (Agarwal and Narain 1991; Sachs and Santarius 2007), the motion also notes that no serious effort has been made to constrain unnecessary luxury consumption.

Emergency measures require a strategy: in secret, AOSIS agree to pool some of their limited tourist revenues, and the delegation from low-lying and especially vulnerable Tuvalu, an island getting rich selling and leasing use of its "tv" internet domain name, makes a generous contribution to hiring a cruise ship from an international tourism corporation. With hundreds of citizens from the island states that are facing inundation safely on board, the ship quietly sets sail for Vancouver. Once there the "tourists" disembark and converge on the few major bridges into and out of the city. There they calmly sit down in the middle of the roadways and block rush-hour traffic, bringing the city to a halt and causing anger and panic among city officials, who call for assistance from provincial and federal agencies. An emergency debate is called in the House of Commons in Ottawa and . . .

Of more concern here, however, is the leaflet circulated by the protestors, and the internet version that rapidly spreads from a series of sites with the "tv" domain name, which justifies the action by quoting Dr Robyn Eckersley's arguments concerning the right of endangered peoples to ecological defense. It points out that the traffic disruption in Vancouver is very much less damaging than the looming inundation of their island states, and that consequently their action is much less than proportional to the harm caused by Canada's violation of its international obligations. The protestors vow to remain on the bridges until the provincial government in Alberta and the federal government in Ottawa permanently cease oil production from the tar sands. A later paragraph on the leaflet explains that Vancouver is after all the place of origin of Greenpeace and non-violent international environmental action, and expresses the hope that the citizens of the city and Canada will thus rally to the cause of the islanders' ecological defense.

This counterexample raises two key points that extend Eckersley's (2007) examination of the limits of ecological intervention. First is that the existing discussion of intervention still remains trapped within the contemporary logic of nation states; this scenario is of course partly guilty of this limitation, too. Climate change and such matters are still considered a matter mainly for state action, and insofar as powerful states have in many cases signally failed to live up to their obligations, the big political question raised by climate change in particular is what other options there might be for ethical action on this matter in light of the need to act to protect the human security of island populations in particular and other peoples and future generations more generally (Barnett 2007). International affairs are no longer only a matter of territorial states and military force, and discussion of ethical action needs to consider other actors including corporations, citizens, NGOs, aid agencies, family networks, and all manner of other communities not constrained by state boundaries.

Second, and related to this, is the question of the ability to act in the international arena. As the scenario here suggests, the actions of civil society might well be understood as another form of "intervention" premised on other definitions of ecological emergency. Suggesting that climate change is not an emergency, because it is not immediate, avoids confronting the consequences of extravagant consumption and once again points the finger of accusation at poorer and marginal states as in need of interventions, rather than looking directly at the larger sources of the biospheric disruptions in the Anthropocene. The inadequacies of the existing state system to deal with these matters once again emphasizes the importance of the broader human security agenda, but also that ethical action in the larger cause of ecological defense will have to overcome the limits of "intervention" as defined in the ICISS framework.

A broader notion of human security is clearly needed to grapple with contemporary changes; but one sensitive to the interconnections between places and the increasingly artificial contexts within which people are vulnerable. But likewise the recognition that vulnerable people are in motion, and will be seen either as victims in need of assistance or as illegal migrants who can be portrayed as a security threat to borders, also poses important questions concerning the adequacy of many states to cope with the disruptions of climate change. Might international migration be an appropriate response for many people in states where their government has obviously failed in its responsibility to protect? Human security isn't only about dealing with people in situ; in present times it is also very much about dealing with people who move to escape environmental changes in the long run and disasters in the short run.

Climate Change and the Military, Again

As chapter 4 showed, much of the debate about environmental change has become subsumed in the discussion of climate change in the first decade of the twenty-first century. Given the far-reaching ramifications of climate change this makes good sense, but it also raises the issue of how security institutions deal with climate and what kind of preparations are being discussed to deal with various scenarios. As chapter 4 suggested, the security scenario in the *GEO4* analysis suggests that security, and the use of force to maintain the status quo, may lead to serious problems and thwart attempts to think about sustainability. However, in the aftermath of the discussions of climate change in the United Nations Security Council in April 2007, numerous studies and reports have emerged that deal with this matter in a more nuanced way. In this section we will deal with just a few high-profile ones to examine the geopolitical formulation of threats and the policy proposals that result from these new specifications of the terrain of danger.

In particular, discussions of migration have frequently invoked geopolitical security narratives in considering the displacements caused by climate change. While some national security documents show an understanding of the importance that numerous aspects of climate change may have for the national security of the United States in particular, not least such things as hurricane damage to military bases (Busby 2007), other views emphasize the disruptions and potential wars caused by migration and enhanced pressure on resources (CNA Corporation 2007; Dan Smith and Vivekananda 2007). The number of people relocated in the aftermath of Hurricane Katrina indicates a pattern that other events will replicate.

> This displacement of tens of thousands of New Orleans (and other Gulf Coast) residents following Hurricane Katrina is symbolic of a larger trend occurring throughout the world. As climate change and its associated processes result in more intense storms, sea level rise or other cataclysmic environmental events, as some scientific studies are predicting, these events are likely to generate large numbers of environmental migrants or refugees. (Paul Smith 2007: 618)

When these migrants are linked to refugee and immigration concerns, and especially to illegal immigration and the potential political problems caused by these people, as has frequently been done in the post-9/11 world, then once again the criminal frame and the security response are deemed necessary. The dangers of this come precisely in circumstances where sudden mass migrations are triggered by disasters. The exodus of more than one hundred thousand people in the summer of 1980 by boat across the Caribbean, or Haitian boat-people setting sail once again, suggests these possibilities.

> Disruptive migration events can be stimulated by wars, civil conflict, economic collapse, natural disasters, famines, or other causes. They tend to be chaotic and, as their name implies, disruptive. When Malaysia faced an influx of thousands of Indonesians fleeing that country's economic crisis in 1998, it responded by implementing a large sea and air operation along the Malacca Straits to deter thousands of illegal immigrants. (Paul Smith 2007: 622)

Criminalizing "illegal" migrants fleeing a disaster suggests not only the possibilities of humanitarian disasters but international tensions, too. The opposite effect happens as well; aiding refugees can frequently improve relations as cooperation and assistance build relationships across frontiers. Ironically, disasters can be diplomatic opportunities when practical cooperation across boundaries increases trust between state functionaries and leaders (Kelman 2007).

Once again the way these events are framed in political terms, as threats requiring a security response, or as responsibilities and opportunities to offer assistance and to improve international cooperation, leads to very different outcomes. European naval patrols in the Mediterranean and in the Atlantic attempting to thwart African migrants desperate to get to Europe is not an encouraging precedent, but the overarching tendency in human affairs is clearly toward increased mobility. This too is part of the accelerated urbanization of the world (Worldwatch Institute 2007); migrants are moving into cities and up the urban hierarchy through the nodes in the global economy. But politics is still frequently about national boundaries, and insofar as xenophobic nationalism is seen as an appropriate policy response to migration, the lot of those dispossessed by disaster or environmental change is made that much more difficult. Human security isn't just about interventions to protect within one country; the responsibility to protect has to incorporate the displaced; existing refugee conventions are in place in part to do this, but environmental displacements suggest that much more needs to be done here.

As Paul Smith (2007) notes, the role of the media in portraying immigrants as a threat and a challenge to the state's authority can play a key role in whether situations are rendered in security terms or in terms of assistance to the displaced. Popular culture too is part of the way the world is portrayed; it too provides a vocabulary for the discussion of environment and other disasters and how states respond. Many of these themes have been explored in recent movies which deal with disasters and responses to them. Climate change was obviously the theme in *The Day After Tomorrow*, the Hollywood blockbuster disaster movie of 2004, but the scenes of American refugees streaming south and attempting to cross into the safety of Mexico were a particularly poignant commentary on the politics of migration. More disturbing is the more recent construction of the category of "fugee" in the dystopic vision of the near future in the movie *Children of Men*, where military means are used to arrest foreigners and deport them from Britain. The television pictures from Gaza in January 2008, as Palestinians dynamited a hole in the wall bordering Egypt to allow people to escape the blockade the Israelis had erected around what had effectively become the largest prison camp on the planet, suggest the security logic of such matters where "different" populations are rendered as a security threat requiring fences and walls to constrain migration. Periodic media reports of India building a fence along the border with Bangladesh suggest a similar security response to migration from that low-lying state as storms render a substantial part of its population vulnerable to sea-level changes.

Clearly the American military is also concerned about migration and instability caused by climate change. In one analysis published in 2007 the situation is summarized in an ominous series of suggestions of how environmental matters may trigger many disruptions.

- Projected climate change will seriously exacerbate already marginal living standards in many Asian, African, and Middle Eastern nations, causing widespread political instability and the likelihood of failed states.
- Unlike most conventional security threats that involve a single entity acting in specific ways and points in time, climate change has the potential to result in multiple chronic conditions, occurring globally within the same time frame. Economic and environmental conditions in already fragile

areas will further erode as food production declines, diseases increase, clean water becomes increasingly scarce, and large populations move in search of resources. Weakened and failing governments, with an already thin margin for survival, foster the conditions for internal conflicts, extremism, and movement toward increased authoritarianism and radical ideologies. (CNA Corporation 2007: 5)

The Centre for Security and International Studies in Washington (Kurt M. Campbell et al. 2007) has also taken this discussion very seriously, drawing experts, including J. R. McNeill, together to examine a number of scenarios for the future. Among the points made in their analyses are the unpredictability of future events, the dangers of scapegoating and violence against minorities in a crisis, and the importance of reconstructing the American energy economy to simultaneously reduce dependence on imported petroleum and slow the emissions of greenhouse gases. The experts note that where organized states are in place, the chances of war over water in particular are very low, but in circumstances where states are not effective, violence might be more likely to occur. In light of the current American preoccupation with "terrorist threats," the dangers of remote areas being rendered ungovernable and hence bases for future "terrorist" organizations also gets discussed in this study.

What is especially clear in these documents is that preparations for dealing with crises are essential, and that prediction of future events is not possible in more than very general terms. In short, the urban context of humanity's existence requires thinking very carefully about security policy and planning for contingencies that may look very different from the military preoccupations of the past. Military notions of security will have to be updated accordingly. But insofar as those peripheral ungoverned places are seen as a threat to the metropolitan centers, and not vulnerable to changes caused by the economies that keep those metropolitan centers functioning, the geopolitical framework driving the "war on terror" is replicated rather than challenged (Dalby 2007b).

Anthropocene thinking suggests that the causalities that matter flow the other way; metropolitan production of greenhouse gases is what is driving climate change, which in turn is disruptive on the periphery. Simply reassembling the security interests left over from the Cold War, to reprise Robert Kaplan's (1994) phrasing of matters from chapter 1, to protect borders and monitor migration doesn't tackle the sources of the disruptions. Such security thinking fails to address the most basic issue of ensuring the necessary conditions for civilization.

Climate Security

The logic of a fundamental rethink of energy and climate security is made especially clear in a recent analysis published by the Royal United Services Institute (RUSI) in London. This report directly confronts the importance of thinking ahead to anticipate potential conflict while moving quickly to de-carbonize economies and reduce the acceleration of the accumulation of greenhouse gases (Mabey 2007). Explicitly invoking the language of prevention, as opposed to the traditional understanding of security to respond to crises, this analysis written by an environmentalist author is significant because it was published as a discussion paper by an institution at the heart of the British military establishment. The analysis points squarely at the need to rebuild infrastructure and economies so that carbon content in the atmosphere is curtailed; this while simultaneously working directly with international institutions to cooperate in anticipating crises and preparing to deal with disruptions. This is not a traditional military response of building armies to deal with aggression, but a policy that takes global change seriously and emphasizes the need to adapt military thinking to deal with the new circumstances.

But given the current circumstances of environmental change, of which climate change is only perhaps the most obvious manifestation, the question of environmental obligations across borders has once again become unavoidable. Emergency circumstances are being invoked by a diverse range of thinkers, from James Lovelock (2006) in his pessimistic analysis in *The Revenge of Gaia*, through discussions of Kunstler's (2006) "long emergency" and peak oil, to the formulation of environmental emergencies by Australian Friends of the Earth (Spratt and Sutton 2008), who invoke the medical term "Code

Red" in their call for immediate action to tackle climate change. But the geopolitics of who should intervene where to stop what kind of environmental threat to whom is a complicated matter when analysis focuses on cases that might justify such actions. Following Lovelock (2006), the Australian Friends of the Earth suggest that the kind of mobilization undertaken in the 1940s during the Second World War is the scale of effort that is now needed to begin reducing greenhouse gases quickly. Now strategists are finally beginning to think similar things.

In language that is not much different from statements that have until recently been dismissed as alarmist when used by environmental groups, Mabey (2007: 1–2) warns that:

> Climate change is like a ticking clock: every increase in greenhouse gases in the atmosphere permanently alters the climate, and we can never move the hands back to reclaim the past. Even if we stopped emitting pollution tomorrow, the world is already committed to levels of climate change unseen for hundreds of thousands of years. If we fail to stop polluting, we will be committed to catastrophic and irreversible changes over the next century, which will directly displace hundreds of millions of people and critically undermine the livelihoods of billions. There is some scientific uncertainty over these impacts, but it is over when they will occur not if they will occur – unless climate change is slowed. Preventing catastrophic and runaway climate change will require a global mobilisation of effort and co-operation seldom seen in peacetime.

Mabey (2007) goes on to comment that the present responses to this future are grossly inadequate, not least because of economic underestimates of the costs of climate disruption as well as the failure to think about the security implications. In military terms, failure to plan for worst-case scenarios for climate change is an abrogation of institutional responsibility by the militaries of many states. Failure to control greenhouse gases will likely have security consequences as grave as the world wars in the twentieth century. For all these reasons, serious policy initiatives are needed immediately, according to this report.

Looking ahead at the likely events that will have security effects, Mabey (2007: 22) divides them into three categories: high-impact events that are reversible, irreversible events, and the third – the nightmare scenario of runaway climate change. In the first category are changes that might be reversible if carbon dioxide is stabilized in the next century, including such things as "shift of Asian monsoons; dramatic weakening of the Atlantic conveyor; large increases in hurricane and typhoon activity; increased drought and flooding cycles; and shifting and productivity reduction in major commercial fisheries" (Mabey 2007: 22). More serious are matters where things cannot be reversed, because they pass points of no return in terms of human timelines, effectively understood in terms of 10,000 years, even if temperatures are stabilized. Such things as "species extinction; alpine glacial melting; and melting of the Greenland and Antarctica ice sheets" (Mabey 2007: 22) fit into this category. Finally there is the prospect of

> Runaway Climate Change: where climate change passes a tipping point where positive feedback loops release more greenhouse gases into the atmosphere from natural sources. At this point humans will lose complete control of climate change and final equilibrium will depend on the interaction of natural systems, for example: release of sub-sea methane hydrates; release of methane from frozen tundra; large scale forest die-back; slowing of ocean CO_2 absorption. (Mabey 2007: 22)

In these circumstances there is little by way of prediction that is helpful in terms of what future human geography might look like, although dubious science fiction novels have long speculated on what such futures might hold. However, drastic scenarios are appropriate in circumstances of runaway change. Perhaps the suggestion made by Australian Friends of the Earth (Spratt and Sutton 2008), that the tropical world becomes uninhabitable and only those parts of Canada, Northern Europe, Greenland, Russia, and Antarctica that remain above the elevated sea levels are available for human habitation by a much reduced population, is a useful guess as to what might transpire.

There is a rich irony in this RUSI report, arguing that politicians are reluctant to think about dramatic and existential challenges to their societies, and that many development workers and environmental activists don't want to discuss the dangers of social collapse because it might invoke an inappropriate securitization, or because of the radical positions on social issues involved that will be quickly dismissed by critics. Mabey (2007) forcefully reiterates an old argument from the 1990s debate (Dalby 1996) that it is precisely the security agencies that are used to dealing with conflict and the worst-case scenario, so they are in fact the best equipped to think through the future threats that climate change is bringing. In addition, Mabey (2007) invokes the ICISS theme of the responsibility to protect as a necessary part of the military's rethinking of security and its protection of societies into the future.

In doing all these things Mabey provides a powerful set of arguments for de-carbonizing developed economies, making climate cooperation a higher foreign policy priority than protecting domestic industry, and working to enhance resource management mechanisms in many places so they can handle shortages and disruptions when they happen. All of which suggests a very different set of priorities from those encapsulated in the *GEO4* scenario that warned of the likely roadblocks to sustainability if security as conventionally practiced was a policy priority. It does so because Mabey (2007) suggests that the seriousness of climate change is such that traditional military thinking is no longer applicable given the existential threat that climate change will pose to contemporary developed societies; unless, that is, things are done very soon to tackle carbon emissions and prepare societies to cope with the changes that are already inevitable because of greenhouse gases that have already been put into the air.

At least some people in London are taking such arguments seriously; the 2008 *National Security Strategy* of the UK is quite as blunt in its assessment of future security threats linked to climate change:

> Climate change is potentially the greatest challenge to global stability and security, and therefore to national security. Tackling its causes, mitigating its risks and preparing for and dealing with its consequences are critical to our future security, as well as protecting global prosperity and avoiding humanitarian disaster. (United Kingdom Cabinet Office 2008: 18)

Clearly the human security agenda focus on prevention is timely here too; policies to prevent conflict and reduce environmental disruption go hand in hand here. Peacebuilding and development are both needed but will have to be worked on as part of a larger package that deals with consumption of fossil fuels in particular in the global economy. If these fail to be incorporated into security thinking and policy in the next few decades, then it is clear that climate change will very fundamentally challenge the security of many states.

Policy and Peacebuilding

Much violence and conflict related in numerous ways to economic and political change has an environmental dimension, but in much of the scholarly literature since the Brundtland commission report (WCED 1987) it seems to be clear that the environment is rarely a direct and immediate cause for violence. The fact that this is the case is key to both the literature on peace parks and the broader discussions of environmental diplomacy and peacemaking (Conca and Dabelko 2002). Precisely because environmental matters are important, but not a direct cause of warfare, there is the possibility of conflict mitigation and peacebuilding. Hence international cooperation on such things as peace parks acts as a confidence-building measure and establishes patterns of cooperation that reduce the likelihood of disputes escalating to warfare (Ali 2007). This may be especially important in Africa, where climate change may yet aggravate numerous political difficulties (Brown et al. 2007).

The point is that in many places environmental cooperation is a useful mode of confidence-building (Bencala and Dabelko 2008). Shared resources usually require complicated arrangements to deal with locale-specific issues. Peace is not imposed by fiat in these conditions, but worked at from the local context to larger institutions (Matthew et al. 2002). Would that the drafters of the Framework Convention on Climate Change, and much more specifically the Kyoto protocol, had understood that overarching global agreements on environmental matters are more likely to be built through a series of bottom-up initiatives rather than an attempt to incorporate everything that is relevant into one formula that can be applied to the whole globe (Prins and Rayner 2007)! Taking seriously the poorest countries' concerns with ecological debt, and their need for human development to reduce their vulnerabilities, are long overdue as starting points for negotiating international agreements on climate change (Kjellen 2008). Doing this starts linking human security directly to the causes of disruptions that make people vulnerable.

Asking the right question in the first place is key to good policy-making, and assuming that the question is clear in advance seems to be one of the key problems bedeviling the scholarly and policy literature on environmental conflict for the last two decades. Kahl's (2006) summary of the environmental conflict literature struggles bravely to encapsulate the whole debate, but at the end the lack of a common understanding is not surprising given the multiplicity of scholarly approaches involved. Precisely what question is posed is crucial, and here, where policy agendas drive research, as they so frequently do, the question of who poses the question and how it fits larger institutional mandates cannot be avoided. Thinking through the connections in commodity chains and the violence that might be averted by international political strategies to manage the commodities is part of the puzzle (Le Billon 2007).

Likewise an explicit focus on peacebuilding here is also relevant; not least because of the fairly robust empirical finding, especially in the investigations of water management, that environmental matters frequently lead to cooperation (Giordano et al. 2005). They do this in part because geographical and physical attributes of rivers and water systems make violent conflict counterproductive for all concerned. Few scholars, and none of the major recent reports on these matters, have concluded that major inter-state wars are likely in the event of climate changes, but the potential for further destabilization and the destruction of lives and livelihoods among the poor grows in all scenarios where policy change in the North is not made to tackle these concerns. In short, tackling metropolitan profligacy has become an essential part of a larger peacebuilding strategy that is designed to facilitate adaptation and cooperation in peripheral places. Parks on the boundaries of states in the developing world are now unavoidably part of the same security equation as the provision of renewable energy sources for Americans.

Where a particular issue lies in the larger ecological flows that are increasingly being modified and redirected by human activities seems to be the key consideration for discussing security or peacebuilding. In the words of Wolfgang Sachs and his colleagues (Sachs and Santarius 2007), a "fair future" requires tracing these connections and simultaneously reducing overconsumption while ensuring sustainable commodity provision in the global economy. Hence, empowering sustainable agriculture and promoting water-conserving modes of agro ecology, while reducing the disruptions caused by huge mining projects, simultaneously tackles poverty in the case of agricultural development and avoids the potential for disruptions that cause conflict over environmental damage and compensation. Thinking in terms of these kinds of ecological flows changes the context for peacebuilding by focusing not just on local institutions, but on the larger economic and ecological connections to conflict and the possibilities of sustainable development directly linked to ecological considerations.

On the largest scale this argument connects up with concerns about warfare in the Middle East and the case for renewable energy reducing American dependence in particular on imports of petroleum. If instead the great powers end up in a series of military struggles for access to petroleum and committing huge amounts of resources to exploiting more supplies rather than converting infrastructure to non-fossil-fuel sources, the potential for conflict grows rapidly (Klare 2008). The green economy argument suggests that de-carbonizing the global economy has the double benefit of reducing the violence over resource extraction and simultaneously reducing the disruptions caused by greenhouse gas emissions and climate change (Paterson and Dalby 2009). Likewise, in the case of disruptions, not being dependent on lengthy supply chains improves resilience. Disconnecting metropolitan reliance on essential petroleum supplies from the periphery is a sustainable security strategy from both ends.

This suggests that peace is about the structures and institutions we build and also about energy consumption, and the links between rural and urban places in an interconnected world. Peacebuilding is literally about building things that are sustainable without having violent repercussions either locally or at a distance. It's about constructing buildings that draw on local materials rather than distant concrete factories, solar energy rather than fossil fuels, and local social survival mechanisms rather than the instant solutions of foreign expert contractors. Such an approach would offer a much more ecologically sustainable mode of providing security than do many of the modernizing modes of development that are still practiced by neo-liberal contractors and state elites. This requires that security be a matter of infrastructure planning, building codes, and fuel-efficiency standards, not the kind of routine practical matters that are usually invoked when discussions of security take place. But this is precisely the point of understanding security as an ecological matter, and globalization as an ecological process that requires attention in the formulations of security policy (Pirages and DeGeest 2004; Leichenko and O'Brien 2008). Linking all this explicitly to cooperation in planning to deal with disasters suggests that there are considerable possibilities for peace despite disruptions (Renner and Chafe 2007).

While there are many innovations in the world that are useful models for the future, there is one place where most Americans in particular are least likely to look for innovation. That's Cuba, often simply dismissed as a Cold War relic. Ironically, in part because of American sanctions, and also because of the end of Soviet petroleum supplies, Cuba has already confronted "peak oil" and an increasingly unstable climate, and done so with relatively little help (Worldwatch Institute 2007). What this small country has achieved suggests that change is possible by challenging the taken-for-granted assumptions that inhibit adaptability. Three developments are noteworthy: First is the simple policy of banning incandescent light bulbs and requiring all electrical light fixtures to be equipped with compact fluorescent or other energy-efficient bulbs. This takes pressure off the electrical grid, and the supplies of expensive imported fuels needed for electricity generation are reduced. Second, faced with a lack of fuel, fertilizer, or GMO technologies, Cuban academics are facilitating practical farming innovations with numerous crop-seed varieties to assess which strains grow most effectively in particular ecological conditions. Drawing on traditional knowledge and information-sharing between farmers and communities, appropriate crops can be grown to adapt to changing ecological conditions. Finally, it is worth noting that a simple but robust arrangement of community-based shelters and emergency planning has allowed Havana and other Cuban cities to survive major hurricanes recently with very little loss of life (Sims and Vogelmann 2002).

Human Security in the Anthropocene

The sheer scale of human activity in the last couple of centuries has changed the context within which humanity exists. The new Anthropocene era is now the appropriate framework to use to understand human security. Combining HUGE and HESP with a consideration of the sources of endangerment, and the inadequacy of existing institutions to cope with the vulnerabilities now obvious in the Anthropocene, starkly presents the dilemmas that face both analysts and policy-makers trying to tackle matters of environmental security. But what is clear from the analysis in this chapter is that the traditional focus on states as protectors is no longer an adequate geo-political specification for what needs to be done; the formulations of human security make this inadequacy unavoidable, and the recognition that equity and impacts do not follow state boundaries reinforces the point (O'Brien and Leichenko 2006), but these insights do not resolve the dilemmas that need urgent attention.

Both the immediate contexts in which people live, and the larger environmental processes that are now increasing the hazards that make people vulnerable in these new urban contexts, are partly caused by humanity's actions. This is very troubling for people still thinking in terms of an external environment as the context for human activities. However, the new ecological circumstances of the Anthropocene indicate that we are collectively shaping our vulnerabilities, both directly in terms of where people live, how they are fed, and how sanitation and other necessities are provided, and indirectly through our changing the biosphere, precisely by the economic activities and the changes to ecosystems that we have set in motion.

Thinking about the sources of environmental dangers, and about the possibilities of international actions to "intervene" in order to promote human security, makes the political dilemmas especially acute. Clearly, it is necessary to start building cities and economies in ways that simultaneously increase resilience and reduce the total artificial throughput in the biosphere, although the sheer diversity of ways this can be incorporated into thinking about municipalities is daunting (F. Dodds and Pippard 2005). There remains the need to act to lift the poorest people out of poverty while not wrecking the remaining ecosystems humanity needs to survive in the long run. Thinking about commodity chains and the ecological impacts of whole production systems has also become essential (Princen et al. 2002). But it is clear that initiatives will have to come from metropolitan consumers, who are in many ways much less vulnerable than the poorest and most marginal people, who have done nothing to cause the ecological disruptions that now both directly and indirectly threaten their human security.

All of which suggests the importance of an ecological interpretation of events and human populations, rather than a top-down, state-centric view of things where the government runs things from the capital city. In James Scott's (1998) terms, "seeing like a state" is in many ways still a problem where urban elites manipulate rural matters for their own enrichment. Ecological metaphors of social organization suggest that adaptability and innovation without control from central government may offer many possibilities. Traditional social networks and marketing arrangements have much to offer in a crisis. But these may be foreclosed, so long as poor urban and rural populations are understood as a security problem that needs to be managed as either a state-building project or as peoples in need of modernization by contemporary neo-liberalism.

Insofar as states and municipal governments provide basic infrastructure, sanitation, a public health system, and a plan for emergency assistance in the event of disaster, the human security of the population is enhanced (Brauch 2005a). But where slum dwellers are understood as threats to political orders that emphasize international markets, and development as the promotion of enclaves of modernity, foreign-based tourism, and commodity exports, then the militarization of development is likely to remain a temptation for state elites. This is all the more so where such strategies can be sold abroad as a contribution to contemporary geopolitical struggles against "terrorism," and remote places inhabited by vulnerable people are mapped as dangerous, ungoverned areas that need military intervention (Galgano 2006).

By now it is clear that the causes of many of the disruptions are not indigenous factors in the South, but rather the global economy and the strategies of the rich and powerful to sustain their current modes of urban consumption. We are increasingly changing those contexts and making artificial connections between people across the globe as we transform the biosphere (Steffen et al. 2004). This new recognition of the interconnectedness of our collective fates has given rise to a discussion of the new geological circumstances of humanity. Now we need to understand the global economy as a new "forcing mechanism" in the biosphere, not something separate from an external "environment." In Bruno Latour's (2007) terms, we need earthly sciences, and a politics that explicitly has policies for such unlikely things as the Gulf Stream, if the ecosystems of the planet are not to be so drastically disrupted as to make civilization as we know it impossible.

Interconnections are key to all this, both between places and between humanity and the biospheric context that we are collectively remaking. This requires taking ecological science and the concept of the Anthropocene much more seriously in how we rethink security, because we are literally building our collective future in a changing biosphere. Our conceptual formulations of both environment and security need considerable updating; traditional notions of warfighting and enemy states are obviously outdated (Kaldor 2005). In light of scientific discussions in earth-system science, it seems that while the poor in the South continue to struggle with matters of sustainable development, the priority for Northern consumers is now one of reversing the Brundtland commission's formulation and focusing instead on the urgent need to "develop sustainability." Putting this at the heart of a security strategy would require abandoning many of the traditional geopolitical premises of security thinking and focusing, instead, on urban life and its supporting global economy in the context of biosphere-scale ecological changes in the Anthropocene.

Conclusion: Anthropocene Security

The concept of the Anthropocene and the mode of analysis from earth-system science function to destabilize the verities of modern dualistic thinking. The Anthropocene indicates the importance of understanding the scale of human activity as a growing part of the biosphere, an entity that is essential to human existence, whose functioning we know little about, but which we are already changing. The assumption that "we" are somehow external to a nature that we have to monitor and administer is no longer tenable in the face of both understandings of globalization and global environmental change, which are, of course, but two sides of the same coin even if they are rarely yet understood in quite this manner.

The necessary shift in mentality requires that politics and administration, not to mention the cultural categories of consuming scientists and administrators, move from adaptation and regulation after the fact to thinking seriously about the design and construction of artifacts that minimize ecological throughput. To put the matter directly: successful ecological engineering is a matter of building useful things that do not need to be regulated. The technical dimensions of all this may actually be easier to tackle than the social dimensions, not least because of the powerful persistence of all sorts of social hierarchies that are marked and perpetuated by consumption practices. Status is about a flashy automobile, ones sold to all of us by their capabilities to go anywhere and conquer, literally in the slogans of advertisers, the most forbidding landscapes (Paterson and Dalby 2006). Understanding the ecological consequences of our actions suggests the extreme folly of such heroic individualism fostered in contemporary commodity culture.

The greatest challenge for both the physical and social sciences is to change simultaneously the managerial mentality and the consumption culture that celebrates human "domination" of nature as a virtue. Both are premised on ontological assumptions of separation that ecological sciences, as well as the so-called postmodern turn in social thinking, recognize as untenable. The most pressing theoretical and practical matters related to the Kyoto protocol and its successor agreements, and recent events in the Middle East, all involve very large conceptual themes. These include political questions of who we now are, and how we might usefully change our identities, and our actions, given the sheer scale of recent anthropogenically induced changes within the biosphere. This is especially important because of the newly recognized importance of the interconnections between parts of that biosphere.

Understanding ourselves primarily as citizen consumers within the boundaries of nation states is a fundamentally misleading conception. Earth-system science and the novel predicament that humanity faces suggest that political assumptions of autonomy at the scale of either the individual or the state are no longer tenable. The liberal assumptions of economic rationality and autonomous consumers on the one hand, and of the imperial conquest of nature to provide the "resources" for this mode of existence on the other, are precisely what has structured the unsustainability of contemporary "civilization." The designation "civilization" also suggests the crucial shift in human activities at the beginning of the Anthropocene: that of urbanization. The consumer identities of SUV drivers and tourists are those of urbanites playing in the rural recreational spaces and using resources from all over the planet to do so. Rather than being rendered insecure by environmental change, this mode of consumption is the environmental change that generates many insecurities among the poor and marginal peoples. Getting this geography clear is essential to practical policy thinking that can be effective in the future.

The contemporary tools of international relations and the focus on national security are often not helpful in understanding these social and political relationships. These knowledges that look to universal explanations of the relationships between environment and conflict are usually urban and modern knowledges, ones that take an imperial view of matters for granted. Combined with satellite imagery and modes of monitoring statistics compiled by states and international agencies, and the assumptions of the inevitability of economic development in terms of the expansion of carboniferous capitalism, these formulations of the resource and environment problematique inevitably downplay the rural, the contextual, and the disruptions inflicted on traditional peoples (Peet and Watts 2004). They do so also within a state cartography, one that draws lines between places, ensuring that civil wars "over there" are not usually a matter of responsibility "in here" in the cities of the metropoles. But as the literature on resource wars now makes clear, the consequences of modes of extraction in distant places are tied into violence, dispossession, and environmental destruction (Bannon and Collier 2003; Jung 2003; Le Billon 2005).

To think in these terms is to challenge the conventional geographies of security and the geopolitical assumptions that democracies are peaceful because they do not go to war with each other and that they provide the appropriate vision of a sustainable and non-violent future. Putting the geography of resource extractions back explicitly into the picture changes the terms in which it is possible to construct both "resources" and "conflict." It also suggests the possibilities of innovation to facilitate less ecologically destructive modes of living. Above all it challenges the taken-for-granted geography of danger as external to the modern spaces of prosperity. In short, it requires a shift away from an understanding of environment as the external context of humanity to a recognition of life as interconnected within a changing biosphere.

This most fundamental cultural shift is not likely to be easy to accomplish, as status in modernity is so frequently defined in terms of the ability to waste things and operate free of natural constraints. Conspicuous consumption is so called because that is precisely what it is. Reversing the value assigned to it requires an inversion of the construction of profligacy as a demonstration of power and virtue if we are to construct a more sustainable future (Dauvergne 2008). This will not be an easy cultural and political task (Spaargaren and Mol 2008), particularly given the persistence of neo-Malthusian themes mapped onto a crude geography of external threat and internal innocence; a cartography of danger dramatically enhanced by the events of September 11 and subsequent narratives of wars on terror, the axis of evil, and rogue regimes (Dalby 2007b). None of these narratives is new; they are part of a long discussion of global security which has gradually seen environmental themes become more important.

In light of the emerging understandings of earth-system science, the traditional geopolitical starting points seem singularly inappropriate, not least because they so frequently simply take the material context of politics for granted. Trying to specify which processes have what effect where and when is always difficult when discussing matters of global change. The point about both climate change and the more explicitly human matters of "globalization" is that while they have a common source, the consequences are geographically diverse and socially inequitable. The geography of all this doesn't facilitate easy mapping of the most important processes that flow through both human and natural systems; they rarely happen neatly within the administrative boxes of states (Magnusson and Shaw 2002). This point is now increasingly recognized by military planners and in discussions of climate change. In one crucial sense the arguments from the "limits to growth" debate in the 1970s have turned out to be correct (Graham Turner 2008); there are limits to one key planetary parameter: the ability of the biosphere to absorb the carbon dioxide that is emitted by global carboniferous capitalism. The suggestion in *A Blueprint for Survival* (Goldsmith et al. 1972) of smaller-scale communities making fewer ecological demands likewise seems to fit with the growing realization that the current global economy is a major environmental innovation that is unsustainable if climate change is taken seriously.

However, the assumptions that usually inform discussions of what is to be done in the face of dramatic changes frequently focus on the need to change government policy, to change the rules, and to enforce management standards within territorial jurisdictions. These matters quickly resolve into matters of technical debate, standards, measurements, evaluations, and assessments based on numerous quantifiable factors that are reported to various authorities; nearly always governments and related inter-governmental agencies. The reduction of matters into technical definitions and administrative procedures is about specifying objects of knowledge and approved and correct procedures for management of things so specified; and security likewise, where borders are patrolled, migrants documented, and hostile forces repelled by numerous technical practices. The assumption that security can be made effective by such practices was powerfully reinforced in recent years by the construction of the American Department of Homeland Security (Mabee 2007). However, in light of climate change such thinking is no longer close to enough to secure societies North or South; it may in fact be counterproductive.

The point about earth-system science is that these narrow technical specifications of parts of the environment for management fail to anticipate the connections between systems and the interactions of various ecological phenomena. They are also modes of regulation and administration that frequently fail to take the total impact of particular activities into consideration precisely in the way they break complex matters down into manageable (literally) pieces. The focus on pollutants and toxicities is necessary but frequently fails to encompass the overall utility of the product, while dealing with the narrow technical parameters of "safety." Engineering criteria more generally deny the importance of the human context in decision-making, an omission that frequently has tragic consequences (Gyawali 2001).

This is, in environmentalist terms, of course, part of a larger political problem in that the overall goals of society are beyond discussion; the market supposedly reveals preferences, the politicians and bureaucrats regulate the more pernicious consequences, and we are all supposedly fulfilled by our purchases. The intense controversies over specific chemicals or facility-siting disputes are, in part, because of the expression of modes of human being and values that are in sharp contrast to economic logic. But the scope of conventional environmental impact hearings and routine regulatory procedures doesn't allow the larger discussion of political aspirations, much less religious or traditional invocations of the inviolate and sacred in specific places (Mackenzie and Dalby 2003).

The point here is not that parts of the problems of environmental change are being ignored; rather it is to emphasize the difficulty of encompassing the totality of these matters in terms that can usefully enter into political discussion either in formal state deliberations or in discussions of international relations. This is to push the limits of conventional assumptions that politics is about who gets what where, and to insist that current circumstances require a larger critical engagement with matters of culture and identity (M. C. Williams 2007), concerns of who we are and, hence, the legitimate forms of activity that "we" undertake. Thinking in terms of the Anthropocene suggests that the categories of "nature," "parks," wilderness, and pollution are simply not adequate for the scale of what needs to be discussed, however necessary they are in the current practices of "management." Adding security into the political discussion requires us to think hard about the future and what is so important that it needs to be secured so that in continues into the future (Dalby 2002).

The terms within which such an "Anthropocene ethics," much less an "Anthropocene security," might be written are currently not obvious. The ontologies of autonomy and separation on the one hand, and mechanical causal principles on the other, are not the conceptual tools we need for a larger debate about what Tim Luke (1997, 1999) calls public ecology. Environmentalist tropes of pristine nature suggest the importance of minimizing alterations of many habitats; but so many habitats are now obviously "artificial" that the invocation of a preservationist ethos is frequently inappropriate if ecology, rather than aesthetics, is considered as the basis for policy prescription. The difficulty here is that ecology is all about change; habitats and species come and go while separations between species, the managerial ethos of orderly landscapes and hygienic tropes, is denied by the boundary-crossing realities of material flows (Levin 1999; Forsyth 2003).

In Christian theological terms, the much-quoted line from Genesis about humanity as having dominion over nature (White 1967) can now simply be read as a statement of fact; this is the point of the Anthropocene. It isn't a matter that can any longer be discussed in terms of its moral implications for the future, or a formulation that theories of animal rights or environmental ethics can discuss in terms of living lightly on the earth; rather, it has become the given context for discussion (Sanderson et al. 2002). In McNeill's (2000) terms from chapter 3, there now is *Something New Under the Sun*. The additional point is that ecology no longer allows us to formulate humanity as separate from nature. This is now simply ontologically impossible; formulations premised on such a dichotomy make no practical sense in light of earth-system science.

The sheer difficulty of thinking intelligently about the biosphere is immense; however, this is what security now requires us to do. There remains considerable difficulty grasping the nuances of connection even with the extraordinary cartography made possible by satellite sensors and geographical information systems. The visualization possibilities of these technologies that may yet work to shift cultural sensibilities are still in their infancy. The view from the satellite is a cartographic representation of the view from above, the "God trick" view. This doesn't necessarily foster a sensibility to connection, contingency, and impermanence of the kind needed to grasp the intricate interconnections and changes in the biosphere (Thomashow 2002). Thinking about ecology in the Anthropocene is not helped by assuming that truth and reality are best understood in terms of permanence, unity, and stability. The difficulties of encompassing such things within practical political action are daunting; perhaps, as Wapner (2003) suggests, we have little choice but to focus on a few items and try to improve matters piecemeal; but these actions have to be shaped by a recognition of the ecological context within which they are taking place to guide our new understanding of security.

The international dimensions of these things still need some clear "ethical" frameworks that suggest priorities in particular places. The key to this is understanding the importance of geographical context, a matter that hopefully the Anthropocene discussions of the flows of materials and energies through changing ecosystems makes easier to see. Universal political strategies are not what is needed in a world of great diversity; general principles will work best when specific contexts are understood as the starting point for practical tasks (Hunold and Dryzek 2002). Where one is situated in the flows should suggest which priorities are most pressing; this is the point of thinking ecologically.

Thinking about both environmental change and security requires us to understand that we live in an interconnected world that we are actively changing. Insofar as we understand security as stability in some senses, we need to understand that the economic system that we are trying to render stable is in fact one of rapid change. Most frequently in security thinking it's the political order that supposedly provides security that is rendered the essential entity that must be secured. But the geopolitical order of major state rivalry that conventional international relations suggests is inevitable is part of the problem when it comes to climate change. Power understood in terms of fossil-fueled industrial weapons systems, and the world understood as inevitably competitive, perpetuate the insecurities that ecology suggests we need to confront. In contrast, sustainable security suggests that both adaptation and mitigation are needed, but implementation requires an approach that combines both so that adaptation is planned while using technologies that mitigate emissions. The solar panel is emblematic of what is needed; it supplies energy with no inputs and no emissions and it can work anywhere there is sunlight, no matter what disasters and disruptions may occur elsewhere.

While technological blueprints should still be resisted, there are some very tentative principles that we can use to think politically. First is the principle that suggests we should operate so as to minimize material throughput in ecosystems. Materials disrupt systems; reducing total throughputs will probably reduce the unknown consequences of our actions (Sachs and Santarius 2007). This is especially so with fossil fuels, where the basic mechanisms of the biosphere are being changed by their use. The second principle is the matter of only making substances that will eventually biodegrade; long-lasting toxins accumulate in food webs and poison unpredictably. Reducing the quantity of toxic substances in our production systems is key in reducing the health impacts of unsustainable production for humans and other beings (Geiser 2001). Third is the precautionary principle that we assume the worst and try to avoid irreversible experiments. There are huge difficulties with this general principle, but the impetus has to be on playing safe in the face of numerous unknowns. The North American native peoples' idea of thinking seven generations ahead when making important decisions is helpful here, even if foresight is much less than perfect (LaDuke 1999). Fourth, one might add the reverse onus principle on the producers of new substances, who must prove the substances actually are safe to use prior to their introduction into ecosystems. Fifth is the principle of sufficiency that recognizes that more is not necessarily better (Princen 2005). This challenges the logic of consumption and the assumption that growth necessarily benefits the majority and is therefore virtuous. In place of efficiency, sufficiency suggests that enough is enough, rather than more is better.

Also needing attention are the more traditional concerns with environment as the rural, the surrounds of the cities, the backdrop to metropolitan life. However, if we follow the first principle above, and reduce material throughputs, some of the pressures on rural lands, waters, and biodiversity will be reduced. But that said, it is clear that a sixth principle is needed that encompasses the crucial point about trying to maintain ecological diversity where at all possible to keep future options open. As the discussion of the Millennium Ecosystem Assessment (2005) in chapter 3 made clear, agriculture has long been a major factor in the disruption of habitat, a category related to Enlightenment notions of wilderness as unproductive and the need to "improve" land to make it valuable. But such dichotomies are now rendered impossible too by Anthropocene thinking. Habitats are key to maintaining ecological diversity and essential to the health of any species; they are real gene banks that facilitate innovation, adaptation, and evolution, unlike the stasis of artificial storage proposed by many technically focused discussions of diversity preservation. But habitats need to be interconnected so that animals, birds, and plants can move and adapt to changing circumstances. Artificial linear barriers like roads, and areal barriers like cities and fields, dangerously compromise mobility for many species. Put together, these principles amount to an ethic of care directed to life, something akin to an ethic of flourishing in Cuomo's (1998) eco-feminist terms.

Anthropocene thinking requires that the contemporary discussions of global change and globalization be merged into one. The flows across boundaries, of people, materials, fuel, and pollution, that are sources of concern to many who study "globalization" are precisely the processes that are forcing the biospheric system in the new ways that so worry earth-system scientists. This pattern makes sense if matters are viewed in terms of the imperial dimensions of global trading, where peripheries supply the raw materials for production plants that provide the commodities for the metropoles. Shadow globalization and the disruptions caused by the expansion of modernity into remote parts of the human world are also an important part of what the destruction of the "wild" is all about (Sanderson et al. 2002).

Insofar as states function to secure consumption and the supplies of resources through the global economy, they are frequently intensifying the changes in the flows of materials through ecological systems. Road-building and the promotion of car culture as a development strategy in many places are only the most obvious manifestation of this political difficulty; states are building the infrastructure that is changing the biosphere. Expecting them to regulate environmental matters effectively so long as this remains their dominant goal is not the basis of either an effective domestic strategy or international regime-building. Intelligent land-use planning remains but a dream in the suburbanization of many places where developers' prerogatives so frequently hold sway in municipal politics (Davis 2002). All these facets of "automobile politics" (Paterson 2007) have to be tackled in the promotion of global public ecology. So too does the role of states in energy provision. Campaigns to revive the nuclear power industry, justified in part by concerns over carbon dioxide emissions from conventional power plants, once again raise security concerns about weapon proliferation and authoritarian states needed to control this technology (Stoett 2003).

The overarching requirements of Anthropocene thinking suggest principles very considerably different from the contemporary focus in neo-liberalism on self-governance, international efficiency, and the whole technocratic panoply of mechanisms of ecological modernization. Tom Princen (2005) suggests that the theme of sufficiency is an essential prerequisite for reforming international environmental governance along lines that take the future seriously. Crucially, he suggests that sufficiency avoids the use of efficiency to export environmental destruction in one place to another. But such ruminations are rather different from traditional considerations of environmental ethics in terms of the rights of animals or duties to endangered species. They also require an explicit recognition that "protecting" the environment is not now a matter of preventing change to aesthetically desirable locations so that they can be continually "enjoyed" in some sense; it's about the global economy and its transformations (Clapp and Dauvergne 2005).

Ecology now isn't about parks and protection as much as it is about changing modes of production and consumption and, inevitably in the process, about challenging the production of the modern identity of the autonomous knowledgeable subject, one free from the constraints of an external nature. As Walker's (2006) analysis in chapter 2 showed, the modern identity based within states and separate from an external nature is key to much of contemporary political thought and practice. This modern subject is also an imperial one, one that is imperious and impervious to the externalized consequences of their actions. A postmodern subject who is conscious of the contingencies and connections of contemporary life is one more likely to understand their own existence as dependent on the flows of resources and materials from distant places, and to understand that the urban environments, and the rural playgrounds that provide leisure experiences, are dependent on resource extractions and population displacements elsewhere.

Such a cultural transition is not going to be easy, but as Michael C. Williams (2007) suggests, security is a matter of symbolic power and crucially a matter of cultures that claim their preservation as the most important matter. Re-imagining ourselves as within a changing biosphere rather than on an earth we can dominate and control is the key to any notion of sustainable security. In Williams' (2007) terms, this is a very different culture from the neo-conservative assumptions that violence and technology can remake the world to ensure the continued triumph of modernity. Linking climate issues to fear and supposing that we can engineer our way out of present difficulties may appear the logical extension of security to environment, but it's not the kind of cultural change that is likely to be very helpful (Hulme 2008).

None of these philosophical reflections would seem to have much to do with how security has traditionally been thought about either in academic thinking or in policy practice by modern states. This is so because the traditional focus on control by dividing up the world into spaces that could be policed by actual or threatened violence is simply out of date in the face of global phenomena (Rogers 2008). Malthusian formulations discussed at the beginning of this book are tremendously dangerous, precisely because they facilitate such control policies while failing to deal with the causes of the disruptions that set people in motion. These theories do so not least because of their inadequate geographical premises. They argue in various ways that threats are from outside, caused by natural phenomena, hence security understood in terms of keeping these threats at bay is appropriate. But this geography is simply wrong.

The Anthropocene formulation makes it clear that humanity is now a major force shaping the biosphere. It challenges the Malthusian formulation because it shows the connections that cross boundaries while also showing that many of the poor and marginal are made so by the environmental processes of the global economy. Consequently security and modern identity must be fundamentally rethought. Indeed, perhaps this book might be better titled "Environment and Security Change"! Putting people rather than states at the heart of the analysis is a HUGE task (Oswald Spring 2008), but one that is necessary to challenge attempts on the part of the prosperous to maintain their privileges in the face of the needs of the poor. The politics of this cannot be evaded forever; perhaps Rogers (2008) is right and the failure of the "war on terror" to accomplish its ostensible aims makes this all the more likely to be understood. Not least, the failures of the Bush doctrine, with its simplistic formulas of enforced regime change and moral clarity (Fred Kaplan 2008), should suggest that politics and security are no longer possible in these terms if either survival for the poor in the short term, or long-term ecological integrity for most of us, is taken seriously.

While the Anthropocene demands that ethical activity engages this politics, it also makes simplistic slogans of "protecting the environment" or unreflective formulations of environmental security much more difficult. As outlined above, this is so because the scale of environmental change is now such that no part of the biosphere is beyond the range of anthropogenic influence. Abandoning the taken-for-granted virtues of environment, and understanding humanity as within ecological processes rather than within cities that are surrounded at a distance by environs, or within metropoles surrounded by "the South," is now necessary in thinking about security. We have to put science and politics together too (Forsyth 2003). In doing so we have to think about politics as the mutual constitution of humanity and nature, rather than considering them as separate spheres (Latour 2004).

The key point about the operation of securitization is precisely that it refers to pressing and immediate situations that normal political life cannot address. In this regard, the invocation of emergencies in present times is important to deal with the climate-change issue and the larger matters of ecological disruption. But as this book has made clear these are not topics that can effectively be tackled by traditional military means; Daniel Deudney's (1990) warning about this remains apt. However, insofar as Mabey's (2007) argument about the seriousness of climate change presenting an existential threat to modern states is clearly in line with the scientific examinations of the Anthropocene, perhaps military warnings about the imminent dangers should societies not set about changing their current trajectory in the short run might be particularly appropriate. In doing so, military warnings will have to confront the traditional divisions between science and politics as well as challenge contemporary geopolitical frameworks and their specification of dangers as originating in peripheral places.

Overcoming these divides, between science and politics, between culture and nature, urban and rural, suggests that we need postmodern subjectivities sensitive to context and to the consequences of differences, places, and connections. These subjectivities suggest the need to build sensibly for the future rather than trying to literally ground politics in protecting things that inevitably change. Working to enhance ecosystems' diversity and fecundity is the key to sustaining lots of things. But similar principles apply to the construction of technologies, buildings, and infrastructure to facilitate their surviving storms (Auerswald et al. 2006).

Responding to disasters and cooperating where and when people are suffering have become the norm in international politics in the last couple of decades. While many states remain highly suspicious of humanitarian interventions and the principle of the responsibility to protect, nonetheless the habits of cooperation and the impulse to assist in the face of disaster offer promising pathways for further cooperation and the recognition that we are common inhabitants of a biosphere first, and citizens of particular states only secondarily. This rethinking of the implicit terms of geopolitics is gradually shifting the terms of international cooperation; extending it in the coming decades will be especially important if security is to respond to environmental change. But if it is simply a re-imposition of liberal forms of modernization, it will fail to produce the cultural innovations focusing on multiple forms of life that are needed (Duffield 2007).

Above all, the invocation of the Anthropocene suggests the need to think simultaneously about connections, the importance of flexibility and adaptability, and the impossibility of complete certainties, while always keeping the inevitability of surprise in mind. It suggests a very different notion of security is needed if ecological thinking structures the categories used to examine what precisely is endangering whom in particular places. The Anthropocene also emphasizes the urgency of immediate action to drastically curtail greenhouse gas emissions for everyone's security, and the need to build both institutions and structures with the future clearly in focus. This is not security understood as preparing for war with rival states. It's security in terms of ecological understandings of humanity as a new presence in a biosphere that we are already changing quite drastically. Environmental change now makes the necessity of rethinking security unavoidable.

References

Abramovitz, Janet N. 2001. *Unnatural Disasters* Washington DC: Worldwatch Institute: Worldwatch Paper 169.

Adams, Jonathon and Thomas O. McShane. 1992. *The Myth of Wild Africa: Conservation without Illusion*. Berkeley: University of California Press.

Adger, Neil. 2006. "Vulnerability." *Global Environmental Change* 16: 268–81.

Agarwal, Anil and Sunita Narain. 1991. *Global Warming in an Unequal World: A Case of Environmental Colonialism*. New Delhi: Centre for Science and Environment.

Ali, Saleem H. (ed.). 2007. *Peace Parks: Conservation and Conflict Resolution*. Cambridge MA: MIT Press.

Alley, Richard B. 2004. "Abrupt Climate Change." *Scientific American* November: 62–9.

Anjaria, Jonathon Shapiro. 2006. "Urban Calamities: A View from Mumbai." *Space and Culture* 9(1): 80–2.

Auerswald, Philip E., Lewis M. Branscomb, Todd M. La Porte, and Erwann O. Michel-Kerjan (eds). 2006. *Seeds of Disaster, Roots of Response: How Private Action Can Reduce Public Vulnerability*. Cambridge: Cambridge University Press.

Bacevich, Andrew. 2005. *The New American Militarism: How Americans Are Seduced by War*. Oxford: Oxford University Press.

Bain, William. 2001. "The Tyranny of Benevolence: National Security, Human Security, and the Practice of Statecraft." *Global Society* 15(3): 277–94.

Bannon, Ian and Paul Collier (eds). 2003. *Natural Resources and Violent Conflict: Options and Actions*. Washington: World Bank.

Barnett, Jon. 2001. *The Meaning of Environmental Security*. London: Zed.

Barnett, Jon. 2005. "Titanic States? Impacts and Responses to Climate Change in the Pacific Islands." *Journal of International Affairs* 59(1): 203–19.

Barnett, Jon. 2007. "The Geopolitics of Climate Change." *Geography Compass* 1(6): 1361–75.

Barnett, Jon and W. Neil Adger. 2007. "Climate Change, Human Security and Violent Conflict." *Political Geography* 26: 639–55.

Barnett, Jon, Simon Lambert, and Ian Fry. 2008. "The Hazards of Indicators: Insights from the Environmental Vulnerability Index." *Annals of the Association of American Geographers* 98(1): 102–19.

Bencala, Karin R. and Geoffrey D. Dabelko. 2008. "Water Wars: Obscuring Opportunities." *Journal of International Affairs* 61(2): 21–33.

Bhagat, R. B., Mohua Guha, and Aparajita Chattopadhyay. 2006. "Mumbai after 26/7 Deluge: Issues and Concerns in Urban Planning." *Population and Environment* 27: 337–49.

Blaikie, Piers, Terry Cannon, Ian Davis, and Ben Wisner. 1995. *At Risk: Natural Hazards, People's Vulnerability and Disasters*. London: Routledge.

Bogardi, Janos J. 2004. "Hazards, Risks and Vulnerabilities in a Changing Environment: The Unexpected Onslaught on Human Security?" *Global Environmental Change* 14: 361–5.

Bohle, Hans Georg. 2007. "Geographies of Violence and Vulnerability: An Actor-Oriented Analysis of the Civil War in Sri Lanka." *Erdkunde* 61(2): 129–46.

Boykoff, Maxwell T. and Jules M. Boykoff. 2004. "Balance as Bias: Global Warming and the US Prestige Press." *Global Environmental Change* 14: 125–36.

Brauch, Hans Günter. 2005a. *Environment and Human Security: Towards Freedom from Hazard Impacts*. Bonn: United Nations University Institute for Environment and Human Security Intersections No. 2/2005.

Brauch, Hans Günter. 2005b. *Threats, Challenges, Vulnerabilities and Risks in Environmental and Human Security*. UNU-EHS Source No. 1/2005.

Brauch, Hans Günter, John Grin, Czeslaw Mesjasz, Pal Dunay, Navnita Chadha Behera, Béchir Chourou, Ursula Oswald Spring, P.H. Liotta, and Patricia Kameri-Mbote (eds). 2008. *Globalisation and Environmental Challenges: Reconceptualising Security in the 21st Century*. Berlin, Heidelberg, New York, Hong Kong, London, Milan, Paris, and Tokyo: Springer.

Briggs, Xavier de Souza. 2006. "After Katrina: Rebuilding Places and Lives." *City and Community* 5(2): 119–28.

Brklacich, Mike and H-G. Bohle. 2006. "Assessing Human Vulnerability to Global Climatic Change" in Eckart Ehlers and Thomas Krafft (eds) *Earth System Science in the Anthropocene: Emerging Issues and Problems*. Berlin, Heidelberg, and New York: Springer, 51–61.

Broda-Bahm, Kenneth T. 1999. "Finding Protection in Definitions: The Quest for Environmental Security." *Argumentation and Advocacy* 35: 159–70.

Brown, Oli, Anne Hammill, and Robert McLeman. 2007. "Climate Change as the 'New' Security Threat: Implications for Africa." *International Affairs* 83(6): 1141–54.

Busby, Joshua W. 2007. *Climate Change and National Security: An Agenda for Action*. New York: Council On Foreign Relations CSR NO. 32.

Busby, Joshua W. 2008. "Who Cares about the Weather? Climate Change and U.S. National Security." *Security Studies* 17: 468–504.

Buzan, Barry and Ole Wæver. 2003. *Regions and Powers: The Structure of International Security*. Cambridge: Cambridge University Press.

Buzan, Barry, Ole Wæver, and Jaap de Wilde. 1998. *Security: A New Framework for Analysis*. Boulder CO: Lynne Rienner.

Campbell, David. 1998. *Writing Security: United States Foreign Policy and the Politics of Identity*. Minneapolis: University of Minnesota Press.

Campbell, Kurt M., Jay Gulledge, J. R. McNeill, John Podesta, Peter Ogden, Leon Fuerth, R. James Woolsey, Alexander T. J. Lennon, Julianne Smith, Richard Weitz, and Derek Mix. 2007. *The Age of Consequences: The Foreign Policy and National Security Implications of Global Climate Change*. Washington DC: Center for Strategic and International Studies.

Carmody, Padraig R. and Francis Y. Owusu. 2007. "Competing Hegemons? Chinese versus American Geo-Economic Strategies in Africa." *Political Geography* 26: 504–24.

Castells, Manuel. 1996–8. *The Information Age: Economy Society and Culture*. 3 vols. Oxford: Blackwell.

Castree, Noel and Bruce Braun (eds). 2001. *Social Nature: Theory, Practice, and Politics*. Oxford: Blackwell.

Chatterjee, Partha and Matthias Finger. 1994. *The Earth Brokers: Power, Politics, and World Development*. London: Routledge.

Chew, Sing C. 2001. *World Ecological Degradation: Accumulation, Urbanization, and Deforestation, 3000 BC –AD 2000*. Walnut Creek CA: Alta Mira.

Cigler, Beverly A. 2007. "The 'Big Questions' of Katrina and the 2005 Great Flood of New Orleans." *Public Administration Review* December: 64–76.

Clapp, J. and P. Dauvergne. 2005. *Paths to a Green World: The Political Economy of the Global Environment.* Cambridge MA: MIT Press.

Claussen, Martin, Victor Brovkin, Reinhard Calov, Andrey Ganopolski, and Claudia Kubatzki. 2005. "Did Humankind Prevent a Holocene Glaciation? Comment on Ruddiman's Hypothesis of a Pre-Historic Anthropocene." *Climatic Change* 69: 409–17.

CNA Corporation. 2007. *National Security and the Threat of Climate Change.* Alexandria VA: CNA Corporation.

Cole, H. S. D., Marie Jahoda, K. L. R. Pavitt, and Christopher Freeman (eds). 1973. *Models of Doom: A Critique of The Limits to Growth.* New York: Universe.

Commission on Global Governance. 1995. *Our Global Neighbourhood.* Oxford: Oxford University Press.

Commission on Human Security. 2003. *Human Security Now.* New York: Commission on Human Security.

Conca, Ken and Geoff Dabelko (eds). 2002. *Environmental Peacemaking.* Washington DC: Woodrow Wilson Center Press.

Cooper, Melinda. 2006. "Pre-empting Emergence: The Biological Turn in the War on Terror." *Theory, Culture and Society* 23(4): 113–35.

Croft, Stuart and Terry Terriff (eds). 2000. *Critical Reflections on Security and Change.* London: Frank Cass.

Cronon, William. 1983. *Changes in the Land: Indians, Colonists and the Ecology of New England.* New York: Hill and Wang.

Crosby, A. 1986. *Ecological Imperialism: The Biological Expansion of Europe 900–1900.* Cambridge: Cambridge University Press.

Crutzen, Paul. 2002. "Geology of Mankind." *Nature* 415: 23.

Cuomo, Chris, J. 1998. *Feminism and Ecological Communities: An Ethic of Flourishing.* London: Routledge.

Curtis, Andrew, Jacqueline Warren Mills, and Michael Leitner. 2007. "Katrina and Vulnerability: The Geography of Stress." *Journal of Health Care for the Poor and Underserved* 18: 315–30.

Dabelko, Geoff. 2008. "An Uncommon Peace: Environment, Development and the Global Security Agenda." *Environment* May/June 50(3): 32–45.

Dalby, Simon. 1996. "Security, Intelligence, the National Interest and the Global Environment" in David A. Charters, Stuart Farson, and

Glenn P. Hasted (eds) *Intelligence Analysis and Assessment* London: Frank Cass. 175–97.

Dalby, Simon. 1997. "Contesting an Essential Concept: Reading the Dilemmas in Contemporary Security Discourse" in Keith Krause and Michael Williams (eds) *Critical Security Studies: Concepts and Cases*. Minneapolis: University of Minnesota Press, and London: Pinter, 3–31.

Dalby, Simon. 2002. *Environmental Security*. Minneapolis: University of Minnesota Press.

Dalby, Simon. 2003. "Geopolitical Identities: Arctic Ecology and Global Consumption." *Geopolitics* 8(1): 181–203.

Dalby, Simon. 2007a. "Geopolitical Knowledge: Scale, Method and the Willy Sutton Syndrome." *Geopolitics* 12(1): 183–91.

Dalby, Simon. 2007b. "Regions, Strategies, and Empire in the Global War on Terror." *Geopolitics* 12(4): 586–606.

Dauvergne, P. 1997. *Shadows in the Forest: Japan and the Politics of Timber in South East Asia*. Cambridge MA: MIT Press.

Dauvergne, P. 2008. *The Shadows of Consumption: Consequences for the Global Environment*. Cambridge MA: MIT Press.

Davis, Mike. 1999. *Ecology of Fear: Los Angeles and the Imagination of Disaster*. New York: Vintage.

Davis, Mike. 2001. *Late Victorian Holocausts: El Niño Famines and the Making of the Third World*. London: Verso.

Davis, Mike. 2002. *Dead Cities*. New York: New Press.

Davis, Mike. 2006. *Planet of Slums*. London: Verso.

De Sherbinin, Alex, Andrew Schiller, and Alex Pulsipher. 2007. "The Vulnerability of Global Cities to Climate Hazards." *Environment and Urbanization* 19(1): 39–64.

De Villiers, Marq. 2008. *Dangerous World: Natural Disasters, Manmade Catastrophes, and the Future of Human Survival*. Toronto: Viking.

Deudney, Daniel.1990. "The Case against Linking Environmental Degradation and National Security." *Millennium* 19: 461–76.

Deudney, Daniel. 1998. "Global Village Sovereignty: Intergenerational Sovereign Publics, Federal-Republican Earth Constitutions, and Planetary Identities" in Karen Litfin (ed.) *The Greening of Sovereignty in World Politics*. Cambridge MA: MIT Press, 299–325.

Deudney, Daniel. 1999a. "Environmental Security: A Critique" in Daniel Deudney and Richard Matthew (eds) *Contested Grounds: Security and Conflict in the New Environmental Politics*. Albany: State University of New York Press, 187–219.

Deudney, Daniel. 1999b. "Bringing Nature Back In: Geopolitical Theory from the Greeks to the Global Era" in Daniel Deudney and Richard Matthew (eds) *Contested Grounds: Security and Conflict in the New Environmental Politics*. Albany: State University of New York Press, 25–57.

Deudney, Daniel and Richard Matthew (eds). 1999. *Contested Grounds: Security and Conflict in the New Environmental Politics*. Albany: State University of New York Press.

Diamond, J. 1997. *Guns, Germs and Steel: The Fates of Human Societies*. New York: Norton.

Diamond, J. 2005. *Collapse: How Societies Choose to Fail or Succeed*. New York: Viking.

Dillon, Michael. 2008. "Underwriting Security." *Security Dialogue* 39(2–3): 309–32.

Dodds, F. and T. Pippard (eds). 2005. *Human and Ecological Security: An Agenda for Change*. London: Earthscan.

Dodds, Klaus. 2008. "Icy Geopolitics." *Society and Space* 26: 1–6.

Duffield, Mark. 2007. *Development, Security and Unending War: Governing the World of Peoples*. Cambridge: Polity.

Dunn, Kevin. 2003. *Imagining the Congo: The International Relations of Identity*. New York: Palgrave Macmillan.

Eckersley, Robyn. 2007. "Ecological Intervention: Prospects and Limits." *Ethics and International Affairs* 21(3): 293–316.

Ehrlich, Paul R. 1968. *The Population Bomb*. New York: Ballantine.

Eikenberry, Angela M., Verónica Arroyave, and Tracy Cooper. 2007. "Administrative Failure and the International NGO Response to Hurricane Katrina." *Public Administration Review* December: 160–70.

Esty, Daniel C. 1999. "Pivotal States and the Environment" in Robert Chase, Emily Hill, and Paul Kennedy (eds.) *The Pivotal States: A New Framework for U.S. Policy in the Developing World*. New York: Norton, 290–314.

Esty, Daniel C., J. A. Goldstone, T. R. Gurr, B. Harff, M. Levy, G. D. Dabelko, P. Surko, and A. N. Unger. 1998. *State Failure Task Force Report: Phase II Findings*. McLean VA: Science Applications International Corporation.

Evans, G., J. Goodman, and N. Landsbury (eds). 2002. *Moving Mountains: Communities Confront Mining and Globalization*. London: Zed.

Fagan, Brian M. 1999. *Floods, Famines, and Emperors : El Niño and the Fate of Civilizations*. New York: Basic Books.

Fagan, Brian M. 2004. *The Long Summer: How Climate Changed Civilization.* New York: Basic Books.

Farazmand, Ali. 2007. "Learning from the Katrina Crisis: A Global and International Perspective with Implications for Future Crisis Management." *Public Administration Review* December: 149–59.

Fierke, K. M. 2007. *Critical Approaches to International Security.* Cambridge: Polity.

Flannery, Tim. 1995. *The Future Eaters: An Ecological History of the Australasian Lands and People.* New York: George Braziller.

Flannery, Tim. 2006. *The Weather Makers: How We Are Changing the Climate and What it Means for Life on Earth.* Toronto: HarperCollins.

Floyd, Rita. 2008. "The Environmental Security Debate and its Significance for Climate Change." *International Spectator* 43(3): 51–65.

Forsyth, Tim. 2003. *Critical Political Ecology: The Politics of Environmental Science.* London: Routledge.

Foster, Gregory D. 2005. "A New Security Paradigm." *Worldwatch Magazine* 18(1): 36–46.

Freudenburg, William R., Robert Graming, Shirley Laska, and Kai T Erikson. 2007. "Katrina: Unlearned Lessons." *World Watch Magazine* September/October: 14–19.

Fussel, Hans-Martin. 2007. "Vulnerability: A Generally Applicable Conceptual Framework for Climate Change Research." *Global Environmental Change* 17: 155–67.

Gadgil, M. and R. Guha. 1995. *Ecology and Equity: The Use and Abuse of Nature in Contemporary India.* London, Routledge.

Galgano, Francis. 2006. "A Geographical Analysis of UN-Governed Spaces." *Pennsylvania Geographer* 44(2): 67–90.

Gedicks, A. 2001. *Resource Rebels: Native Challenges to Mining and Oil Corporations.* Boston: South End.

Geiser, Kenneth. 2001. *Materials Matter: Toward a Sustainable Materials Policy.* Cambridge MA: MIT Press.

Gelinas, Nicole. 2007. "Baghdad on the Bayou." *City Journal* Spring, www.city-journal.org/html/17_2_new_orleans.html.

George, Susan. 1988. *A Fate Worse than Debt.* Harmondsworth: Penguin.

German Advisory Council on Global Change. 2008. *Climate Change as a Security Risk.* London: Earthscan.

Giordano, Mark, F. Meredith, A. Giordano, and Aaron T. Wolf. 2005.

"International Resource Conflict and Mitigation." *Journal of Peace Research* 42(1): 47–65.

Giroux, Henry A. 2006. "Reading Hurricane Katrina: Race, Class, and the Biopolitics of Disposability." *College Literature* 33(3): 171–96.

Gleditsch, Nils Petter, Kathryn Furlong, Havard Hegre, Bethany Lacina, and Taylor Owen. 2006. "Conflicts over Shared Rivers: Resource Scarcity or Fuzzy Boundaries?" *Political Geography* 25: 361–82.

Goldsmith, Edward and editors of the *Ecologist*. 1972. *A Blueprint for Survival*. Harmondsworth: Penguin.

Goucha, Moufida and John Crowley (eds). 2008. *Rethinking Human Security*. Oxford: Wiley-Blackwell.

Graham, Stephen. 2006. "Cities Under Siege: Katrina and the Politics of Metropolitan America." Social Science Research Council, http://understandingkatrina.ssrc.org.

Graham, Stephen. 2009. *Cities Under Siege: The New Military Urbanism*. London: Verso.

Green, Rebekah, Lisa K. Bates, and Andrew Smyth. 2007. "Impediments to Recovery in New Orleans' Upper and Lower Ninth Ward: One Year after Hurricane Katrina." *Disasters* 31(4): 311–35.

Grove, Richard. 1995. *Green Imperialism: Colonial Expansion, Tropical Island Edens, and the Origins of Environmentalism, 1600–1800*. Cambridge: Cambridge University Press.

Grove, Richard. 1997. *Ecology, Climate and Empire: Colonialism and Global Environmental History, 1400–1940*. Cambridge: White Horse.

Grundmann, Reiner. 2007. "Climate Change and Knowledge Politics." *Environmental Politics* 16(3): 414–32.

Gunderson, Lance H. and C. S. Holling (eds). 2002. *Panarchy: Understanding Transformations in Human and Natural Systems*. Washington DC: Island Press.

Gupta, Kapil. 2007. "Urban Flood Resilience Planning and Management and Lessons for the Future: A Case Study of Mumbai, India." *Urban Water Journal* 4(3): 183–94.

Gyawali, Dipak. 2001. *Water in Nepal*. Kathmandu: Himal Books.

Haag, Fredrik and Flora Hajdu. 2005. "Perspectives on Local Environmental Security, Exemplified by a Rural South African Village." *Environmental Management* 36(4): 483–94.

Haider-Markel, Donald P., William Delehanty, and Matthew Beverlin.

2007. "Media Framing and Racial Attitudes in the Aftermath of Katrina." *Policy Studies Journal,* 35(4): 587–605.

Hampson, Fen Olser, Jean Daudelin, John B. Hay, Holly Reid, and Todd Marting. 2002. *Madness in the Multitude: Human Security and World Disorder.* Toronto: Oxford University Press.

Hansen, James, Makiko Sato, Reto Ruedy, Ken Lo, David W. Lea, and Martin Medina-Elizade. 2006. "Global Temperature Change." *Proceedings of the National Academy of Sciences* 103(30): 14,288–93.

Hartmann, B., B. Subramaniam, and C. Zerner (eds). 2005. *Making Threats: Biofears and Environmental Anxieties.* Lanham MD: Rowman and Littlefield.

Harvey, David. 1974. "Population, Resources, and the Ideology of Science." *Economic Geography* 50(3): 256–77.

Harvey, David. 2003. *The New Imperialism.* Oxford: Oxford University Press.

Hecht, Suzanna and Alexander Cockburn. 1990. *The Fate of the Forest: Developers, Destroyers, and Defenders of the Amazon.* Harmondsworth: Penguin.

Hochschild, Adam. 1998. *King Leopold's Ghost: A Story of Greed, Terror, and Heroism in Colonial Africa.* Boston: Houghton Mifflin.

Homer-Dixon, Thomas. 1999. *Environment, Scarcity, and Violence.* Princeton NJ: Princeton University Press.

Homer-Dixon, Thomas. 2006. *The Up Side of Down: Catastrophe, Creativity, and the Renewal of Civilization.* Toronto: Knopf.

Hornborg, Alf, J. R. McNeill, and Joan Martinez-Alier (eds). 2007. *Rethinking Environmental History: World System History and Global Environmental Change.* Plymouth: Altamira Press.

Hulme, Mike. 2008. "The Conquering of Climate: Discourses of Fear and their Dissolution." *Geographical Journal* 174(1): 5–16.

Human Security Center. 2005. *Human Security Report.* New York: Oxford University Press.

humansecurity-cities.org. 2007. *Human Security for an Urban Century: Local Challenges, Global Perspectives.* http://humansecurity-cities.org.

Hunold, Christian and John S. Dryzek. 2002. "Green Political Theory and the State: Context is Everything." *Global Environmental Politics* 2(3): 17–39.

Independent Commission on Population and Quality of Life. 1996. *Caring for the Future.* Oxford: Oxford University Press.

Intergovernmental Panel on Climate Change. 2007. *Climate Change*

2007: Synthesis Report. Geneva: IPCC. www.ipcc.ch/pdf/assessment-report/ar4/syr/ar4_syr.pdf.

International Commission on Intervention and State Sovereignty. 2001. *The Responsibility to Protect*. Ottawa: IDRC.

International Geosphere Biosphere Programme. 2001. "Global Change and the Earth System: A Planet Under Pressure." *IGBP Science* No. 4.

Jackson, Robert. 2000. *The Global Covenant: Human Conduct in a World of States*. Oxford: Clarendon.

Jacques, Peter J., Riley E. Dunlap, and Mark Freeman. 2008. "The Organisation of Denial: Conservative Think Tanks and Environmental Scepticism." *Environmental Politics* 17(3): 349–85.

Jung, Dietrich. 2003. *Shadow Globalization, Ethnic Conflicts and New Wars: A Political Economy of Intra-State War*. London: Routledge.

Jurkiewicz, Carole L. 2007. "Louisiana's Ethical Culture and its Effect on the Administrative Failures Following Katrina." *Public Administration Review* December: 57–63.

Kahl, Colin. 2006. *States, Scarcity, and Civil Strife in the Developing World*. Princeton NJ: Princeton University Press.

Kaldor, Mary. 2005. "Old Wars, Cold Wars, New Wars, and the War on Terror." *International Politics* 42: 491–8.

Kaldor, Mary. 2007. *New and Old Wars: Organized Violence in a Global Era*. 2nd edn. Stanford CA: Stanford University Press.

Kaplan, Fred. 2008. *Daydream Believers: How a Few Grand Ideas Wrecked American Power*. Hoboken NJ: John Wiley.

Kaplan, Robert D. 1994. "The Coming Anarchy." *Atlantic Monthly* 273(2): 44–76.

Karim, M. F. and N. Minura. 2008. "Impacts of Climate Change and Sea-Level Rise on Cyclonic Storm Surge Floods in Bangladesh." *Global Environmental Change* 18(3): 490–500.

Kearns, G. 2009. *Geopolitics and Empire: The Legacy of Halford Mackinder*. Oxford: Oxford University Press.

Kelman, Ilan. 2007. "Hurricane Katrina Disaster Diplomacy." *Disasters* 31(3): 288–309.

Kjellen, Bo. 2008. *A New Diplomacy for Sustainable Development: The Challenge of Global Change*. New York: Routledge.

Klare, Michael. 2004. *Blood and Oil: The Dangers and Consequences of America's Growing Dependency on Imported Petroleum*. New York: Metropolitan Books.

Klare, Michael. 2008. *Rising Powers/ Shrinking Planet: The New Geopolitics of Energy.* New York: Metropolitan Books.

Klein, Naomi. 2007. *Shock Doctrine: The Rise of Disaster Capitalism.* New York: Knopf.

Korf, Benedikt. 2005. "Rethinking the Greed–Grievance Nexus: Property Rights and the Political Economy of War in Sri Lanka." *Journal of Peace Research* 42(2): 201–17.

Korf, Benedikt. 2006. "Cargo Cult Science, Armchair Empiricism and the Idea of Violent Conflict." *Third World Quarterly* 27(3): 459–76.

Kunstler, James Howard. 2006. *The Long Emergency: Surviving the End of Oil, Climate Change, and Other Converging Catastrophes of the Twenty-First Century.* New York: Grove/Atlantic.

LaDuke, Winona. 1999. *All Our Relations: Native Struggles for Land and Life.* Cambridge MA: South End.

Lamb, H. H. 1995. *Climate, History, and the Modern World.* London: Routledge.

Latour, Bruno. 2004. *Politics of Nature: How to Bring the Sciences into Democracy.* Cambridge MA: Harvard University Press.

Latour, Bruno. 2007. "A Plea for Earthly Sciences." Lecture to the annual meeting of the British Sociological Association East London, April, www.bruno-latour.fr/articles/article/102-BSA-GB.pdf.

Le Billon, Philippe. 2005. *Fuelling War: Natural Resources and Armed Conflict.* Oxford: Routledge for the International Institute of Strategic Studies, Adelphi paper 373.

Le Billon, Philippe. 2007. "Fatal Transactions: Conflict Diamonds and the (Anti)Terrorist Consumer" in Derek Gregory and Allan Pred (eds) *Violent Geographies: Fear, Terror, and Political Violence.* New York: Routledge, 133–52.

Leichenko, R. and K. O'Brien. 2008. *Double Exposure: Global Environmental Change in an Era of Globalization..* New York: Oxford University Press.

Levin, Simon. 1999. *Fragile Dominion: Complexity and the Commons.* Reading MA: Perseus.

Levy, Marc. 1995. "Is the Environment a National Security Issue?" *International Security* 20: 35–62.

Linden, Eugene. 2007. *The Winds of Change: Climate, Weather and the Destruction of Civilizations.* New York: Simon and Schuster.

Liotta, P. H. and James F. Miskel. 2008. "Towards an Ethical Framework for Security" in Hans Günter Brauch, John Grin, Czeslaw Mesjasz, Pal Dunay, Navnita Chadha Behera, Béchir

Chourou, Ursula Oswald Spring, P.H. Liotta, and Patricia Kameri-Mbote (eds) *Globalisation and Environmental Challenges: Reconceptualising Security in the 21st Century*. Berlin, Heidelberg, New York, Hong Kong, London, Milan, Paris, and Tokyo: Springer, 879–86.

Lipschutz, Ronnie. 1997. "Environmental Conflict and Environmental Determinism: The Relative Importance of Social and Natural Factors" in Nils Petter Gleditsch (ed.) *Conflict and the Environment*. Dordrecht: Kluwer, 35–50.

Lipschutz, Ronnie. 2004. *Global Environmental Politics: Power, Perspectives, and Practice*. Washington DC: CQ Press.

Lohmann, L. 2005. "Malthusianism and the Terror of Scarcity" in B. Hartmann, B. Subramaniam, and C. Zerner (eds) *Making Threats: Biofears and Environmental Anxieties*. Lanham MD: Rowman and Littlefield, 81–98.

Lohmann, L. (ed.). 2006. *Carbon Trading: A Critical Conversation on Climate Change, Privatisation and Power*. Development Dialogue No. 46, www.dhf.uu.se/publications.html.

Lomborg, Bjorn. 2001. *The Skeptical Environmentalist: Measuring the Real State of the World*. Cambridge: Cambridge University Press.

Lonergan, Steve. 2001. "Water and Conflict: Rhetoric and Reality" in Paul F. Diehl and Nils Petter Gleditsch (eds.), *Environmental Conflict*. Boulder CO: Westview, 109–24.

Lovelock, James. 1979. *Gaia: A New Look at Life on Earth*. Oxford: Oxford University Press.

Lovelock, James. 2006. *The Revenge of Gaia: Why the Earth is Fighting Back – and How We Can Still Save Humanity*. London: Allen Lane.

Luke, Timothy W. 1997. *Ecocritique: Contesting the Politics of Nature, Economy, and Culture*. Minneapolis: University of Minnesota Press.

Luke, Timothy W. 1999. *Capitalism, Democracy, and Ecology: Departing from Marx*. Champaign: University of Illinois Press.

Mabey, Nick. 2007. *Delivering Climate Security: International Security Responses to a Climate Changed World*. London: Royal United Services Institute, Whitehall Paper No. 69.

Mackenzie, Fiona and Simon Dalby. 2003. "Moving Mountains: Community, Nature and Resistance in the Isle of Harris, Scotland, and Cape Breton, Canada." *Antipode* 35(2): 309–33.

Magnusson, Warren and Karena Shaw (eds). 2002. *A Political Space: Reading the Global through Clayoquot Sound*. Montreal and Kingston: McGill Queen's Press.

Makhijani, Arjun and Kevin R. Gurney. 1995. *Mending the Ozone Hole: Science, Technology, and Policy*. Cambridge MA: MIT Press.

Malthus, Thomas. 1970 (original 1798). *An Essay on the Principle of Population*. Harmondsworth: Penguin.

Mander, J. and E. Goldsmith (eds). 1996. *The Case Against the Global Economy, and for a Turn to the Local*. San Francisco: Sierra Club Books.

Marchak, P. 1995. *Logging the Globe*. Montreal and Kingston: McGill-Queens University Press.

Marsden, William. 2007. *Stupid to the Last Drop: How Alberta is Bringing Environmental Armageddon to Canada (and Doesn't Seem to Care)*. Toronto: Knopf.

Masozera, Michel, Melissa Bailey, and Charles Kerchnerc. 2007. "Distribution of Impacts of Natural Disasters Across Income Groups: A Case Study of New Orleans." *Ecological Economics* 63: 299–306.

Mathews, Jessica T. 1989. "Redefining Security." *Foreign Affairs* 68(2): 162–77.

Matthew, Richard, Mark Halle, and Jason Switzer (eds). 2002. *Conserving the Peace: Resources, Livelihoods and Security*. Winnipeg: International Institute for Sustainable Development.

MccGwire, Michael. 1991. *Perestroika and Soviet National Security*. Washington DC: Brookings Institution.

McNeill, J. R. 2000. *Something New Under the Sun: An Environmental History of the Twentieth-Century World*. New York: Norton.

McNeill, J. R. 2005. "Diamond in the Rough: Is There a Genuine Environmental Threat to Security? A Review Essay." *International Security* 30(1): 178–95.

McNeill, J. R. 2007. "Yellow Jack and Geopolitics: Environment, Epidemics, and the Struggles for Empire in the American Tropics, 1640–1830" in Alf Hornborg, J. R. McNeill, and Joan Martinez-Alier (eds) *Rethinking Environmental History: World System History and Global Environmental Change*. Plymouth: Altamira Press, 199–217.

Meadows, D. H., D. L. Meadows, J. Randers, and W. W. Behrens III. 1974. *The Limits to Growth*. London: Pan.

Millennium Ecosystem Assessment. 2005a. *Synthesis Report*. www.millenniumassessment.org.

Millennium Ecosystem Assessment. 2005b. *Ecosystems and Human Wellbeing*. 5 vols. Washington DC: Island Press.

Mitchell, J. K. 2006. "Urban Disasters as Indicators of Global
    Environmental Change: Assessing Functional Varieties of
    Vulnerability" in Eckart Ehlers and Thomas Krafft (eds) *Earth
    System Science in the Anthropocene: Emerging Issues and Problems*.
    Berlin, Heidleberg, and New York: Springer, 135–52.
Monbiot, George. 2006. *Heat: How to Stop the Planet from Burning*.
    London: Penguin.
Mooney, Chris. 2007. *Storm World: Hurricanes, Politics and the Battle
    Over Global Warming*. Orlando FL: Harcourt.
Mumford, Lewis. 1934. *Technics and Civilization*. New York: Harcourt.
Myers, Norman. 1989. "Environment and Security." *Foreign Policy* 47:
    23–41.
Nel, Philip and Marjolein Righarts. 2008. "Natural Disasters and the Risk
    of Violent Civil Conflict." *International Studies Quarterly* 52: 159–85.
Neocleous, Mark. 2008. *Critique of Security*. Edinburgh: Edinburgh
    University Press.
Neumayer, Eric and Thomas Plumper. 2007. "The Gendered Nature
    of Natural Disasters: The Impact of Catastrophic Events on
    the Gender Gap in Life Expectancy, 1981–2002." *Annals of the
    Association of American Geographers* 97(3): 551–66.
Nordhaus, Ted and Michael Shellenberger. 2007. *Break Through: From
    the Death of Environmentalism to the Politics of Possibility*. Boston:
    Houghton Mifflin.
O'Brien, Karen and Robin Leichenko. 2006. "Climate Change, Equity
    and Human Security." *Die Erde* 137: 165–79.
O'Lear, Shannon and Paul Diehl. 2007. "Not Drawn to Scale:
    Research on Resource and Environmental Conflict."
    Geopolitics 12(1): 166–82.
O'Riordan, Timothy. 1976. *Environmentalism*. London: Pion.
Oswald Spring, Ursula. 2008. *Gender and Disasters. Human, Gender
    and Environmental Security: A HUGE Challenge*. Bonn: UNU-EHS,
    Intersection.
Oswald Spring, Ursula, Hans Günter Brauch, and Simon Dalby.
    2009. "Linking Anthropocene, HUGE and HESP: Fourth Phase
    of Environmental Security Research" in Hans Günter Brauch,
    Ursula Oswald Spring, John Grin, Czeslaw Mesjasz, Patricia
    Kameri-Mbote, Navnita Chadha Behera, Béchir Chourou, and
    Heinz Krummenacher (eds) *Facing Global Environmental Change:
    Environmental, Human, Energy, Food, Health and Water Security
    Concepts*. Berlin, Heidelberg, and New York: Springer.

Paterson, Matthew. 2007. *Automobile Politics: Ecology and Cultural Political Economy*. Cambridge: Cambridge University Press.

Paterson, Matthew and Simon Dalby. 2006. "Empire's Ecological Tyreprints." *Environmental Politics* 15(1): 1–22.

Paterson, Matthew and Simon Dalby. 2009. "Over a Barrel: Cultural Political Economy and 'Oil Imperialism'" in François Debrix and Mark Lacy (eds) *The Geopolitics of American Insecurity: Terror, Power and Foreign Policy*. New York: Routledge, 181–96.

Peet, Richard and Michael Watts (eds). 2004. *Liberation Ecologies: Environment, Development and Social Movements*. 2nd edn. New York: Routledge.

Pelling, Mark. 2003. *The Vulnerability of Cities: Natural Disasters and Social Resilience*. London: Earthscan.

Peluso, Nancy and Michael Watts (eds.). 2001. *Violent Environments*. Ithaca NY: Cornell University Press.

Pirages, Dennis Clark and Theresa Manley DeGeest. 2004. *Ecological Security: An Evolutionary Perspective on Globalization*. Lanham MD: Rowman and Littlefield.

Princen, Thomas. 2005. *The Logic of Sufficiency*. Cambridge MA: MIT Press.

Princen, Thomas, Michael Maniates, and Ken Conca (eds). 2002. *Confronting Consumption*. Cambridge MA: MIT Press.

Prins, Gwyn (ed.). 1993. *Threats Without Enemies: Facing Environmental Insecurity*. London: Earthscan.

Prins, Gwyn and Steve Rayner. 2007. "Time to Ditch Kyoto." *Nature* 449(25 October): 973–5.

Prins, Gwyn and Robbie Stamp. 1991. *Top Guns and Toxic Whales: The Environment and Global Security*. London: Earthscan.

Renner, Michael. 1989. *National Security: The Economic and Environmental Dimensions*. Washington DC: Worldwatch Institute, Worldwatch Paper No. 89.

Renner, Michael. 1996. *Fighting for Survival: Environmental Decline, Social Conflict and the New Age of Insecurity*. New York: Norton.

Renner, Michael. 2002. *The Anatomy of Resource Wars*. Washington DC: Worldwatch Institute, Worldwatch Paper No. 162.

Renner, Michael and Zoe Chafe. 2007. *Beyond Disasters: Creating Opportunities for Peace*. Washington DC: Worldwatch Institute.

Risbey, James S. 2008. "The New Climate Discourse: Alarmist or Alarming?" *Global Environmental Change* 18: 26–37.

Roberts, J. Timmons and Bradley C. Parks. 2007. *A Climate of Injustice:*

Global Inequality, North–South Politics, and Climate Policy. Cambridge MA: MIT Press.

Rogers, Paul. 2008. *Why We're Losing the War on Terror*. Cambridge: Polity.

Ross, Eric B. 1998. *The Malthus Factor: Poverty, Politics, and Population in Capitalist Development*. London: Zed.

Ross, Michael. 2004. "What do we Know about Natural Resources and Civil War?" *Journal of Peace Research* 41(3): 337–56.

Rothschild, Emma. 1995. "What Is Security?" *Daedalus* 124(3): 53–98.

Ruddiman, William F. 2003. "The Anthropogenic Greenhouse Era Began Thousands of Years Ago." *Climatic Change* 61(3): 261–93.

Ruddiman, William F. 2005. *Plows, Plagues, and Petroleum: How Humans Took Control of Climate*. Princeton NJ: Princeton University Press.

Ruether, Rosemary Radford. 2006. "After Katrina: Poverty, Race and Environmental Degradation." *Dialog: A Journal of Theology* 45(2): 176–83.

Sachs, Wolfgang and Tilman Santarius (eds). 2007. *Fair Future: Resource Conflicts, Security and Global Justice*. London: Zed.

Sagan, Carl and Richard Turco. 1990. *A Path Where No Man Thought: Nuclear Winter and the End of the Arms Race*. New York: Random House.

Said, Edward. 1979. *Orientalism* New York: Vintage.

Salehyan, Idean. 2008. "From Climate Change to Conflict? No Consensus Yet." *Journal of Peace Research* 45(3): 315–26.

Sandbach, Francis. 1980. *Environment, Ideology, Policy*. Oxford: Blackwell.

Sanderson, Eric W, Malanding Jaiteh, Marc A. Levy, Kent H. Redford, Antoinette V. Wannebo, and Gillian Woolmer. 2002. "The Human Footprint and the Last of the Wild." *BioScience* 52(10): 891–904.

Sassen, Saskia. 2006. *Territory, Authority, Rights: From Medieval to Global Assemblages*. Princeton NJ: Princeton University Press.

Schellnhuber, H. J., P. J. Crutzen, William C. Clark, and J. Hunt. 2005. "Earth System Analysis for Sustainability." *Environment* 47(8): 11–25.

Schneider, Stephen. 1989. *Global Warming: Are We Entering the Greenhouse Century?* San Francisco: Sierra Club Books.

Schneider, Stephen. 2004. "Abrupt Non-Linear Climate Change, Irreversibility and Surprise." *Global Environmental Change* 14(3): 245–58.

Schwartz, Peter and Doug Randall. 2003. "An Abrupt Climate Change

Scenario and its Implications for United States National Security."
October, www.ems.org/climate/pentagon_climatechange.pdf.

Scott, J. C. 1998. *Seeing Like a State: How Certain Schemes to Improve
the Human Condition Have Failed*. New Haven CT: Yale University
Press.

Shapiro, Michael. 1997. *Violent Cartographies: Mapping Cultures of
War*. Minneapolis: University of Minnesota Press.

Shepherd, J. Marshall and Thomas Knutson. 2007. "The Current
Debate on the Linkage Between Global Warming and Hurricanes."
Geography Compass 1(1): 1–24.

Simpson, Adam. 2007. "The Environment–Energy Security Nexus:
Critical Analysis of an Energy 'Love Triangle' in South East Asia."
Third World Quarterly 28(3): 539–54.

Simpson, Jeffrey, Mark Jaccard, and Nic Rivers. 2007. *Hot Air:
Canada's Climate Change Challenge*. Toronto: McLelland
and Stewart.

Sims, Holly and Kevin Vogelmann. 2002. "Popular Mobilization
and Disaster Management in Cuba." *Public Administration and
Development* 22(5): 389–400.

Singer, J. David and Jeffrey Keating. 1999. "Military Preparedness,
Weapon Systems and the Biosphere: A Preliminary Impact
Statement." *New Political Science* 21(3): 325–43.

Smil, Vaclav. 2003. *The Earth's Biosphere: Evolution, Dynamics and
Change*. Cambridge MA: MIT Press.

Smith, Dan and Janani Vivekananda. 2007. *A Climate of Conflict:
The Links between Climate Change, Peace and War*. London:
International Alert.

Smith, Paul J. 2007. "Climate Change, Mass Migration and the Military
Response." *Orbis* 51(4): 617–33.

Smith, Steve. 2005. "The Contested Concept of Security" in Ken Booth
(ed.) *Critical Security Studies and World Politics*. Boulder CO:
Lynne Rienner, 27–62.

Soroos, Marvin. 1997. *The Endangered Atmosphere*. Columbia:
University of South Carolina Press.

Spaargaren, Gert and Arthur P. J. Mol. 2008. "Greening Global
Consumption: Redefining Politics and Authority." *Global
Environmental Change* 18(3): 350–9.

Spratt, David and Philip Sutton. 2008. *Climate Code Red: The Case
for a Sustainability Emergency*. Fitzroy: Australian Friends of the
Earth.

Steffen, W., A. Sanderson, P. D. Tyson, J. Jäger, P. A. Matson, B. Moore III, F. Oldfield, K. Richardson, H. J. Schellnhuber, B. L. Turner, and R. J. Wasson. 2004. *Global Change and the Earth System: A Planet under Pressure*. Berlin, Heidelberg, and New York: Springer.

Steffen, W., P. Crutzen, and J. R. McNeill. 2007. "The Anthropocene: Are Humans Now Overwhelming the Great Forces of Nature?" *Ambio* 36(8): 614–21.

Stoett, Peter. 2003. "Toward Renewed Legitimacy? Nuclear Power, Global Warming and Security." *Global Environmental Politics* 3(1): 99–116.

Sullivan, Sian. 2000. "Getting the Science Right, or Introducing Science in the First Place" in P. Stott and S. Sullivan, (eds) *Political Ecology: Science, Myth and Power*. London: Arnold, 66–90.

Thomashow, Mitchell. 2002. *Bringing the Biosphere Home: Learning to Perceive Global Environmental Change*. Cambridge MA: MIT Press.

Thompson, M. 1998. "The New World Disorder: Is Environmental Security the Cure?" *Mountain Research and Development* 18: 117–22.

Tucker, Richard P. 2007. *Insatiable Appetite: The United States and the Ecological Degradation of the Tropical World*. 2nd edn. Lanham MD: Rowman and Littlefield.

Turco, R. P., O. B. Toon, T. P. Ackerman, J. B. Pollack, and C. Sagan. 1983. "Nuclear Winter: Global Consequences of Multiple Nuclear Explosions." *Science* 222: 1283–92.

Turner, B. L, Roger E. Kasperson, Pamela A. Matson, James J. McCarthy, Robert W. Corell, Lindsey Christensen, Noelle Eckley, Jeanne X. Kasperson, Amy Luers, Marybeth L. Martello, Colin Polsky, Alexander Pulsipher, and Andrew Schiller. 2003. "A Framework for Vulnerability Analysis in Sustainability Science." *Proceedings of the National Academy of Sciences* 100(14): 8074–9.

Turner, Graham. 2008. "A Comparison of the Limits to Growth with 30 Years of Reality." *Global Environmental Change* 18(3): 397–411.

United Kingdom Cabinet Office. 2008. *The National Security Strategy of the United Kingdom*. London: HMSO.

United Kingdom Treasury Department. 2007. *Stern Review Report on the Economics of Climate Change*. Cambridge: Cambridge University Press.

United Nations Development Program. 1994. *Human Development Report 1994*. New York: Oxford University Press.

United Nations Development Program. 2007. *Human Development Report 2007-2008. Fighting Climate Change: Human Solidarity in a Changing World*. New York: United Nations.

United Nations Environment Program. 2007. *GEO4 Global Environmental Outlook: Environment for Development*. Nairobi: United Nations Environment Program.

United Nations High-Level Panel on Threats, Challenges and Change. 2004. *A More Secure World: Our Shared Responsibility*. New York: United Nations.

United Nations International Strategy for Disaster Reduction. 2004. *Living with Risk: A Global Review of Disaster Reduction Initiatives*. Geneva: United Nations.

United Nations International Strategy for Disaster Reduction. 2007. *Disaster Risk Reduction: Global Review 2007*. Geneva: United Nations.

Urdal, Henrik. 2005. "People vs. Malthus: Population Pressure, Environmental Degradation, and Armed Conflict Revisited." *Journal of Peace Research* 42(4): 417–34.

Urry, John. 2008. "Governance, Flows and the End of the Car System" *Global Environmental Change* 18(3). 343–9.

Vandentorren, Stephanie, Florence Suzan, Sylvia Medina, Mathilde Pascal, Adeline Maulpoix, Jean-Claude Cohen, and Martine Ledrans. 2004. "Mortality in 13 French Cities During the August 2003 Heat Wave." *American Journal of Public Health* 94: 1518–20.

Vanderheiden, Steve. 2008. *Atmospheric Justice: A Political Theory of Climate Change*. Oxford: Oxford University Press.

Vellinga, Michael and Richard Wood. 2002. "Global Climatic Impacts of a Collapse of the Atlantic Thermohaline Circulation." *Climatic Change* 54: 251–67.

Walker, R. B. J. 2006. "On the Protection of Nature and the Nature of Protection" in Jef Huysmans, Andrew Dobson, and Raia Prokhovnik (eds) *The Politics of Protection: Sites of Insecurity and Political Agency*. London: Routledge, 189–202.

Walton, Grant and Jon Barnett. 2008. "The Ambiguities of 'Environmental' Conflict: Insights from the Tolukuma Gold Mine, Papua New Guinea." *Society and Natural Resources* 21: 1–16.

Wapner, P. 2003. "World Summit on Sustainable Development: Towards a Post-Jo'burg Environmentalism." *Global Environmental Politics* 3(1): 1–10.

Ward, Barbara and Rene Dubos. 1972. *Only One Earth: The Care and Maintenance of a Small Planet*. Harmondsworth: Penguin.

Weaver, Andrew. 2008. *Keeping our Cool: Canada in a Warming World*. Toronto: Penguin.

Weiss, Thomas. 2007. *Humanitarian Intervention*. Cambridge: Polity.

White, Lynn. 1967. "The Historical Roots of our Ecological Crisis." *Science* 155: 1203–7.

Williams, G. 1995. "Modernizing Malthus: The World Bank, Population Control and the African Environment" in J. Crush (ed.) *Power of Development*. London: Routledge, 158–75.

Williams, Michael. 2007. "The Role of Deforestation in Earth and World-System Integration" in Alf Hornborg, J. R. McNeill, and Joan Martinez-Alier (eds) *Rethinking Environmental History: World System History and Global Environmental Change*. Plymouth: Altamira Press, 101–22.

Williams, M. C. 2003. "Words, Images, Enemies: Securitization and International Politics." *International Studies Quarterly* 47: 511–31.

Williams, M. C. 2007. *Culture and Security: Symbolic Power and the Politics of International Security*. London: Routledge.

Wolf, Eric. 1982. *Europe and the People Without History*. Berkeley: University of California Press.

World Commission on Environment and Development. 1987. *Our Common Future*. Oxford: Oxford University Press.

Worldwatch Institute. 2005. *State of the World 2005: Redefining Global Security*. New York: Norton.

Worldwatch Institute. 2007. *State of the World 2007: Our Urban Future*. New York: Norton.

Xenos, Nicholas. 1989. *Scarcity and Modernity*. London: Routledge.

Yergin, Daniel H. 1977 *Shattered Peace: The Origins of the Cold War and the National Security State* Boston: Houghton Mifflin.

Yergin, Daniel H. 1991. *The Prize: The Epic Quest for Oil, Money, and Power*. New York: Simon and Schuster.

Zalasiewicz, M. C., A. Smith, T. L. Barry, A. L. Coe, P. R. Bown, P. Bentchley, D. Cantrill, A. Gale, P. Gibbard, F. J. Gregory, M. W. Hounslow, A. C. Kerr, P. Pearson, R. Knox, J. Powell, C. Waters, J. Marshall, M. Oates, P. Rawson, and P. Stone. 2008. "Are We Now Living in the Anthropocene?" *GSA Today* February 18(2): 4–8.

Zhang, David D., Peter Brecke, Harry F. Lee, Yuan-Qing He, and Jane Zhang. 2007. "Global Climate Change, War, and Population Decline in Recent Human History." *Proceedings of the National Academy of Sciences* 104(49): 19214–19.

Index

Africa, 18, 25, 27, 31, 33, 60, 62–4, 67, 74, 83, 87, 91, 94–5, 101, 152
agriculture, 18, 33, 45, 59, 60, 62, 70, 71, 76, 81, 83–4, 87, 91, 93–4, 107, 154
Amazon, 21, 23, 102, 103
Anthropocene, 96, 99, 100, 103, 105–6, 112, 126–7, 129, 130–1, 139, 143, 147, 156, 158–60, 164–5, 167–8, 170–2
Arctic, 31, 75, 86, 87, 102, 136
Asia, 27, 60, 73, 74–5, 87, 91, 95, 101–2, 110
Atlantic Ocean, 15, 26, 31–2, 60, 87, 101, 145, 150
atmosphere, 20, 23, 37, 65, 69, 78, 80–1, 95, 97–99, 103–4, 139, 148–50
Australia, 31, 117

Bangladesh, 26, 27, 43, 140, 146
barbarians, 16
beaver, 60–1
biodiversity, 15, 80–2, 84, 91, 93–4
Brauch, Hans Günter, 7, 112, 127, 134, 157

Brazil, 21, 65
Britain, 20, 64, 68, 70, 73, 146
Brundtland Commission, 22, 25, 80–1, 152, 158
Bush, George W., 28, 48, 88
Bush Doctrine, 47, 178

California, 65, 70, 117, 118
Canada, 29, 62, 64, 140–2, 150
carbon dioxide, 20, 69, 81, 95, 98–9, 103, 150, 162, 168
carboniferous capitalism, 77, 99, 130, 136, 160, 162
Caribbean, 110, 145
Chernobyl, 14, 22, 23, 39, 137
Chertoff, Michael, 122
China, 33, 65, 66, 69, 70, 75, 101
Christian, 58, 60, 164
Christianity, 21, 49
civilization, 15, 17–8, 32–4, 38, 49, 61, 67–8, 99, 148, 158, 160
climate, 25, 28, 30, 74, 85, 94, 100, 111, 142–3, 146, 148–52
coal, 28, 68, 70, 94, 99
Cold War, 14, 23–6, 36–42, 44, 48–9, 51, 55–6, 129, 148, 155
Colonization, 56, 60, 71, 100